T0130191

About to be a Dad!

Yiannis Parassiris

authorHOUSE®

AuthorHouse™
1663 Liberty Drive
Bloomington, IN 47403
www.authorhouse.com
Phone: 1-800-839-8640

Published by AuthorHouse 7/31/2012

ISBN: 978-1-4772-1558-6 (sc)
ISBN: 978-1-4772-1559-3 (e)

Contact the writer at parasirisi@gmail.com

Introduction

$\mathcal{T}$his book, if one can call it a book, is written by a man with no experience in book-writing and no writer's training. The reason I started it was, mainly, to put down the intense emotions, of almost unbearable joy and responsibility that flood inside me when I think that in some time from now, God willing, I will be a father for the first time.

You would call it more of a diary than a book. Its purpose is also to show the children that I will possibly have something that they would never have a chance to know, my emotional chaos during the period of expecting their birth. One could say: " All right, if you are feeling this way, what about the poor mother who will be carrying the baby and will be observing her body and soul change in ways and forms that she would never have imagined?" And my answer would be: "I don't know, you tell me!". This is one of the reasons why I admire women and would never want to be one.

Finally, I am writing it for all those fathers that no one ever pays any attention to. No one ever asks how they feel about the fact that they are going to bring a little person into this world, a little person that will depend on them. No one ever cares if their knees get weak when this young creature looks at them with the most innocent eyes ever seen and they ask to be protected and taken care of by a family unit in which they need to feel safe from both external and internal dangers. Just because we have the most fun part in the conception and pregnancy period, must we be subject to indifference from those around us? Guess what? No, we are not all insensitive pigs! Some of us are fully aware of our actions and our responsibilities.

The big Question….

Before I proceed in recording those that I have said I would, I would like to pose a question. I am asking myself, my fantastic wife (there is no luckier husband than me), my parents and my in-laws who have gone through as many things as they have seen and have managed to raise us so masterly, my brother and his wife who have also gone through a lot and have taken many hits and my brother-in-law who I consider to be a very smart and fair man.

Furthermore, I dare pose this question to teams of scientists all over the world and distinguished philosophers of life and existence. Ready?

How is it possible that something so common to everyone, like the birth of a child, be at the same time an extraordinary miracle for each and every one of us? Everyone can give life to a child, or almost everyone, and, of course, this is necessary for the perpetuation of our species, so almost everyone experiences it. How can something so commonplace bring you so close to God, creating feelings that you think that no one else in the world can experience but you?

There is some food for thought!

At this point, I would like to make clear that I am referring to both biological and adoptive parents and I am not referring to people who bear or raise children for any other reason but of only the miracle of life and the privilege of raising a human being.

June 2009

June 1ˢᵗ 2009

The time is approaching that my wife and I are going to start trying to conceive a mini-person. "It is about time" is what I could almost hear my parents and Rena's parents say if they read these lines right now. Rena is my wife…and much more than that. It is true that we have held them back for quite a long time because they were expecting to have become grandparents earlier.

Why the hold-up? Many are the reasons! The primary one was that Rena was still not feeling ready to become a mother. I totally respect that and I appreciate it as it indicates maturity and a thirst for life. We both wanted to enjoy life without any children for a while and by that I mean to be free to travel, to dine in luxurious restaurants, to go clubbing and to Greek "bouzoukia" and do other fun stuff that a childless couple can do. As soon as Rena felt ready to become a mummy and as soon as she accepted the fact that her favorite, gorgeous, God-like Greek performer would not leave his wife and child for her, she announced to me her decision to have a baby!

Well, now it is me that does not want to! Only kidding, of course I do! However, I am a Virgo, thus very organized and plan-oriented, and I need to secure that both of us are working before we take the big step. Rena is a doctor and until she starts her residency, which means that she will be getting paid on a regular basis for at least 4 years, I do not want to go ahead with having a baby. Her appointment is coming soon though and her career as a General doctor (family doctor) is about to commence. She did work up until now but in different positions, always as a doctor, for a limited period each time.

The timing is right for her appointment because I am 35 years old (not yet, in September) and I am starting to feel that the line between my child calling me "daddy" or "grandpa" is starting to become very thin! On the other hand, medicine has made great advances and I am sure that I will live to be a very old man so that I can meet my grandchildren. Maybe it was this insecurity of mine that pushed me to join the gym and consume most of the fruits and vegetables that are produced in the North Eastern Aegean Ocean.

June 3rd 2009

We live in Samos, a beautiful island in eastern Greece. It is a true paradise, especially when we have spent all our lives living in Athens. It was a life decision for me and Rena, a decision we made 4 years ago and, fortunately, have not regretted. It took us quite some time to manage to relocate because of work. Eventually, I found work that appealed to me and….goodbye Big City for good!

It is certain that we vacillated a lot before we made the

final decision that we wanted to move to Samos but, for me, the definitive thought that tipped the scale towards the island of Pythagoras and exquisite sweet wine was the upbringing of our future children. How would I explain later on to my children that we had the choice to raise them on an island that provides all the facilities and amenities of a small town and unparallel natural beauty at the same time and, nevertheless, we chose to raise them in the suffocating environment of Athens?

Rena and I have not yet discussed of exactly when we are going to start trying to create a baby boy or a baby girl. We are, both, very tired, fed up mostly, and very stressed out due to some unpleasant events that took place at Rena's work. I will not get into details so as not to embarrass top political personalities of the island. So, she quit and now she feels much better.

I think the main reason we have not mentioned it to each other yet is that we are both processing the thought, each one of us separately. We understand that the time has come and we are preparing ourselves psychologically.

June 6ᵗʰ 2009

We are in Athens today in order to attend Rena's graduation. For the past 2 years she has been attending seminars of medical acupuncture and on Saturday she is getting her certificate. She was always interested in it and as soon as she realized that acupuncture can now be practised by actual doctors, she immediately signed up for the seminars.

Since I was going to be in Athens, I had arranged to meet my good friend Alexander. Apart from wanting to see him to catch up, I wanted to ask him a few questions about how he perceives fatherhood and the raising of a child.

Alexander has a gorgeous daughter in Elementary school and is one of those fathers that their daughters fall in love with. We first met in an organic products fair 3 years ago. He then used to work for a winemaker who also produced organic cheese. Alexander was in charge of promoting the cheese in the greater area of Athens. The wines of Samos and the wines of this winemaker are distributed by the same company, so I went up to him to introduce myself. In fairs it is quite common to get acquainted with colleagues you may not know, especially those who are closer to your stand. It is a great opportunity to make business contacts that may be found useful in the future and sometimes, like in our case, a simple acquaintance may lead to a nice friendship.

I was finally disappointed because Alexander was so tired from his work that is quite demanding as far as work hours are concerned that he had to cancel. I tried to throw him into a guilt trip arguing that I came all the way from Samos and he cannot spare a couple of hours to see me but when I saw that it was going to work and he was about to give in, I felt guilty myself for pressuring him and I let him off the hook. It doesn't matter, I can't be angry because, in other cases, he always goes out of his way to take me out and entertain me when I am in Athens.

In a way, we are each other's confidants. I was interested in his opinion on what it means to be a father and how he feels about the whole thing. He has seen a lot in his life and he has been through several situations, bad situations, of those that can lead you to dead ends. However, he managed to appreciate the meaning and value of family and he headed towards what most of us consider conventional. His "conventional" ceases to be ordinary and boring and develops into something that leads him to happiness and fulfillment.

August 2009

August 28th 2009

*I*t has been a long time since I have felt the need to write, I guess due to the summer and the feeling of carefree that it brings along with it. Every August, friends and relatives from Athens come to Samos to spend their holidays, so we are occupied with them. After work we meet them at the beach, for lunch or dinner, for evening walks alongside the port and, more or less, we take a mini vacation along with them. Our August is always marked by our friends from Athens and by the acquaintances we make with most of the restaurant owners in Samos.

Food for us, as original Greeks, is not only a form of entertainment but also a chance for contemplation. It seems that on empty stomachs we cannot solve the international problems that occupy the news columns daily. However, when we sit around the table over plates of nioki or farfalle accompanied by Ceasar's salad and a bottle of red Nebiolo vintage 2005, everything is, magically, discussed and solved. Of course, let us not forget the local delicacies such as chickpea balls or stuffed lamb back or fried cheese, etc. accompanied by the aromatic dry wines of Samos. In this case, the issues that are discussed are those that remain within the national borders such as education, high taxation and all those that have been unanswered for decades.

Therefore, since August to us means friends, beaches, romantic strolls and nice dinners, we decided that we wouldn't try to conceive this period so that, in case Rena got pregnant straight away, she wouldn't have the vomiting and all the other disturbing symptoms of the happy event.

September 2009

September 5th 2009

$\mathcal{I}$ woke up this morning soaked in cold sweat. August is over, September is here and the holidays are over. Our friends are gone, no more swimming every day, no more strolls by the seaside. A few days ago, I received the test results that confirm that all is well and that I am healthy enough to multiply myself. Is it time that Rena and I get serious and become parents?

At noon, while Rena and I were driving towards the beach for one of the final swims, just the two of us now, I asked her:

- Baby, what shall we do? Should we get started on having a baby?
- Ahh…yeah…let's…
- So you wanna start making love without protection?
- Ahh..yes…

- As of when?
- As of next time.
- Ohh…ok then…You think the water will be calm today? It is not windy!
- I think so! I hope so; it has been a long time since the beach has been calm.

All right, I admit that the conversation was a bit awkward, but it was a start. After all, it is not an easy decision to make!

I do not want to get into too many details, for obvious reasons, but on the same day we started what we had been preparing ourselves for so long. The feeling is incredible! The freedom given when you don't use protection is redeeming, almost sacred. Personally, I felt that we had just elevated our relationship two steps higher in the ladder of maturity and complete acceptance of each other.

I am such an avid fan of the use of condoms that this is probably the reason why the difference was so intense for me. To me it is a given that the use of condoms should be directly linked to any steady, or not, sexual relationship and should be used every time. There is absolutely no reason for it not to be used. Who can you trust these days? Are you prepared for the consequences? An unwanted pregnancy is the least that can happen to you. Diseases that will hunt you down for a lifetime or even take away your life are not worth a moment of pleasure.

October 2009

October 10th 2009

𝒜 month later and we are sill trying. It would be ridiculous of me to be upset when Rena told me that she got her period. Surely, I cannot expect for us to conceive right away and I know this well. It would be very selfish and pompous of me to believe that we will have good news so fast when other couples try for years and don't make it, leading them to adoption or to submitting their bodies to a series of procedures.

To be honest, though, I did get upset. Maybe not so much upset as my ego was hurt. Apparently, I thought that my sperm would be so quick and supple that there would be no way that at least one of them would not manage to penetrate the attractive ovum which, of course, was impatiently waiting to come face to face with my "runners". I am very arrogant sometimes and I seem to be one of those people that think "this will never happen to me!". I shouldn't though, I should know better. The past few years the problem of infertility has touched my life twice, within my family and my friends.

Manolis, a dear cousin of mine, is married to Maria and they have a son, Thodoris. Thodoris is named after his grandfather, whom he didn't have a chance to meet, but surely Manolis and Maria will talk to him about him. Thodoris is a child that will receive a lot of love in his life. There was no way that he would receive such love from his biological parents. Manolis and Maria's sad fortune of not being able to have their own child turned out lucky for him. They adopted Thodoris and they put him in their lives giving him the right to receive all this repressed desire to raise a child.

I remember my mother telling me, shaken, what Maria had told her" "Aunt, I sometimes just sit and stare at him. I stare at him and cry…". I remember my father telling me that Manolis sings to him to calm him down and help him sleep. "Yiannis, I had no idea that Manolis had had such a wonderful voice!" Had he, had he always had such a great voice or did his vocal cords soften up when the gift of fatherhood was given to him? Or is this wonderful voice coming out from somewhere else?

We must have inside us a secret hiding place in which our talents and our good selves are hiding. The way to find this hideaway is initially to know what you want. The next step in this quest is to find a way to get what you want. Once you finally make it, the code to open it is the word "happiness". And when it is open, you will see coming out all those elements of yourself that can make us great!

I met Laskarina in Junior High through mutual friends. We have been friends ever since, buddies. I don't know how to express it; it is something more than friendship. Which is the word that describes a relationship of total acceptance and understanding? The communication we have surpasses the limits of friendship and is almost turned into a family relation. Laskarina always knew what she wanted and always knew how to get it. She is an example of someone who understands the essence of life, her own life and how she defines it. She is married to Marios, a great guy, a real man. Talking to Marios, even for a little while, you can immediately tell that he is an honest, decent man. What is more touching is the way that he looks at Laskarina, it is obvious in his eyes that he is happy to have her..

On the day that Laskarina told me that they have been trying for 3 years to have a baby and that she had already had an unsuccessful artificial insemination I initially held it together in front of her. We talked about all the medical reasons that could be causing the problem. When I found the nerve to ask her how she is feeling, I think that for the first time since we met she wasn't able to answer clearly.

- How does this make you feel?
- Well, not so well.
- Marios?
- The same.
- Are you stressed about it?
- Quite, and this is a great inhibitor.
- But it is normal to think about it. Unfortunately, it must be a vicious circle, the longer the time goes by, the more stressed you guys must be during sex.
- Exactly!
- I know it is hard, although I 've not been there, but I imagine that you must relax since there is no medical reason.

Laskarina told me what went wrong in the first insemination and how optimistic she is about the second one that has been scheduled. The second one should have already been performed but she got sick and she wasn't allowed to go ahead with it. It has been postponed for November along with her hopes.

That night, I cried myself to sleep. I had never seen Laskarina so weak before. I could feel her agony and the sense of control that she no longer had and it was like someone had stuck a knife in me. It killed me that she was so hurt that she couldn't express her pain, especially when this woman is normally in complete control of her emotions. I can't stand watching my friends so down. And when I think how she must be feeling inside, how much she would like to hold a baby in her arms, to take care of it and spoil it, I feel helpless myself, too, wanting to find a solution for her and being completely unable to do so.

On the other hand, I am glad that she couldn't completely open up to me and tell me how her very soul hurts because that means that she vents with Marios, her husband, her companion. And that is how it should be. Open communication is the best medicine in such cases.

So, now we wait for the second insemination. I hope it all goes well. I pray and beg God that they are not given any more heartache, they don't deserve it. My thoughts are with them. Some people are meant to bring children into this world. I am not saying that there are some who shouldn't because that would be an insult. However, it is also an insult when children are raised in dysfunctional families by people who never really wanted them in the first place.

October 30th 2009

This morning, while driving to work with Rena, she complained to me that she didn't really feel like eating her grilled cheese toast that I had so skillfully wrapped up for her and that she was feeling a bit sick to her stomach. A couple of days ago at home, she was very hungry at night when we had had a very good lunch. Usually, she has the above symptoms a few days before she gets her period but these days she is in the middle of her cycle and they are not justified. Maybe she has a healthier appetite because the temperature is falling; winter is slowly approaching. And she often feels sick to her stomach in the car but now she is a bit dizzy too, it is slightly different. You think…?

With Rena being in the middle of her cycle and her egg being at its best now, the efforts are more intense, although I don't think that our motives are exactly the same. I am calculating the days and I know that they are more favourable now and…how can I say it…I am in a constant "awakening". Rena, on the other hand, is driven by her natural instincts which, due to being in the middle of her cycle, push her to choose her mate and make her more responsive to my suggestions. It is also helpful the fact that my in-laws are away for a few days and we have been completely alone the past four days, which doesn't happen too often. .

When I say that our motives are different, I mean that Rena is more relaxed and is not as anxious as I am. Being a doctor, she understands much better than I do the circumstances under which a woman can get pregnant. She knows that it is a combination of factors and some couples take longer than others. The other day, I opened up a discussion with her so that she can explain a few things to me:

- – Rena, can I ask you something?
- – Yes.
- – In case we have some sort of problem and we can't conceive, how can we find out?

- Yiannis, are you stressed already? Why am I asking? You are, I knew it.
- I am not exactly stressed; what is so wrong with knowing what we could do?
- It is too early to consider the option of getting tested. After all, don't you remember the last time that I saw my gynecologist? He told me that I am anatomically perfect, only 3% of the female population is.   .
- So, then, I may have the problem…
- What "problem" darling, this is not an issue yet.
- All right, I agree with you but why would it matter if next time I go to Athens I went to get tested?
- Because it is still too early!
- Yeah but why not know now something that we could know a year from now? This way we won't waste time and we can react instantly.
- You do have a point there but I don't know where you could go, we can find out. For you, it won't be so difficult, it is for us women that testing is time consuming and hard, too many tests and too expensive.
- That is why I will get tested first and then we will see.
- All right already, let's just wait and see!
- So I will have to visit a clinic and give my sperm?
- You are so stubborn, you are already there! Relax a little!

She was right, I know!
A little while ago, a married couple we know, good

friends of ours, had a very painful experience. They were trying to have a baby and the girl got pregnant. They were very happy as they thought the time was right for them.

However, a few days later the girl had a little blood down there and she was alarmed. They went to the hospital and did all the necessary tests. The doctor told them that she had an ectopic pregnancy. Sadly, they were twins. Surgery had to be performed to remove the embryos. They went through the whole thing on their own, we found out after it had all been over. When they told us, they had already passed through all the stages of loss and they had accepted the fact, mostly, anyway. We were shocked. We couldn't believe that a thing like that could happen to such dear friends.

Rena explained to her that it is simply a matter of luck and it could happen to any woman. What seems like a simple statistic, though, can bring on a lot of pain. You may suddenly become a simple statistic that confirms research that has been done by certified scientists, but the trauma left in one's soul cannot be measured and valued exactly.

December 2009

December 25th 2009

*M*erry Christmas to all! Merry Christmas to the whole world!

Today it is December 25th, 2009! It is Christmas and my Rena has to work at the hospital. It is the first time in 9 years that we won't be together on Christmas Day. What can you do? Some patient will be grateful that Rena will be on guard at the hospital. In this way some family will spend their festive days with their minds at ease. Hopefully, there will be no real need for her.

The scenery today in some homes will be very different from some other ones.

In some homes, mom and dad will get up and will prepare a rich breakfast, warm coffee and melomakarona (Greek sweets with honey customary for Christmas) for the adults and warm chocolate with milk and grilled cheese sandwiches for the kids. The parents will make efforts to wake up the youngsters and they will be saying "oh come on…let us sleep in…no school today…" Some top level negotiations later, the whole family will be gathered around the kitchen table wearing their fluffy pyjamas and planning the rest of the day. If the kids are still young, the activities will include dressing well and warmly and heading outside to a playground or at grandma's and grandpa's house who will anxiously be waiting for all three generations to celebrate the birth of Jesus Christ. If the kids are not kids but teenagers…well…things are a bit different here. Their priority will be their friends and getting together with them for coffee and chit chat. The only thing you can do in this case is to announce the time of the next gathering around the table, where milk and grilled cheese sandwiches will have been replaced by well-cooked meats and overstuffed poultry accompanied by plenty of wine and soft drinks and hope that they come on time.

Beautiful pictures of family bliss! Surely such are the pictures that Loukia and Stamatis must be imagining. Loukia is a childhood friend of Rena's from the notorious gang of four, Rena, Maria, Loukia, Olga. Loukia and Olga are sisters, Rena and Maria are cousins and best friends. The four of them together could be a TV series or an example to all of us of what childhood friendships should be like. They have grown up in the same area, they were even vacationing all together every summer as their parents all know each other. If someone was able to gather the energy that is created when the four of them are together, they could solve the planet's energy supply problem.

Loukia and Stamatis started trying to have a baby around the same period that we did. A couple of months ago, the Four were all in Athens talking and Loukia was worried because she hadn't got pregnant yet. Stamatis was more worried actually because the efforts were quite… frequent and intense…if you know what I mean! But

3 days after Rena came back to Samos they called us and gave us the good news. So we will all expect the first one of the Four to bring a very lucky baby into this world in the middle of July.

In some other homes, the Christmas setting will be very different

Mom and Dad will wake up after the children will because the previous night they had gone out to a friend's house or to a club and they will obviously have one hell of a hangover. Breakfast will consist of cigarettes and strong coffee for the grownups and for the children…whatever is in the fridge; "help yourselves you little pains in the ass…". The older son will try to find a way to hide the bruise on his face. You see, he had the nerve to be awake when dad and mom came back last night (I forgot to mention that the kids were home alone on Christmas Eve while their parents were shaking it in some club) and because dad had a little too much to drink he decided to knock some sense into his son by punching him. It wasn't the first time, of course, the only problem is that this time he can't hide it easily, damn it!

The younger daughter will be up, too, and she will cling on to her brother, as she always does. She will go to the kitchen first to say "good morning" to mommy and daddy but I guess the music last night was too loud and there is something wrong with their ears because they can't hear her and they don't respond to her. The cloud of smoke in the kitchen is too thick and that is probably why they cannot see her also. When she coughs, however, because she has not learned passive smoking very well yet, her mother gets a bit annoyed and says to her with overflowing love: "What the hell are you doing here?…make something to eat and go watch a cartoon or something…and tell that loser brother of yours to turn down the music cause my head hurts". As she is leaving the kitchen, happy that her mother finally noticed her and gave her her Christmas wishes, she passes by her father's side of the table. She stands back a bit…from afar…and looks at him.

She stands back a bit…from afar…and remembers the last day of school before the Christmas holidays. All the children were beautifully dressed and had to recite their poem or sing or act in a little Christmas play. The young girl of our story is a little talent but only her teacher knows it. She sang at the school's Christmas celebration but only her teacher was there to support and admire her. She was so moved because her little student sang the birth of Jesus as if she were an angel. While she was watching her, she thought: "Why can't my husband and I have an angel like this one in our lives to make it magical?...I wonder where her parents are…they didn't show up again…my God what a heavenly voice!…but I can always detect a hint of pain in the voice of my little one…it must be her timbre…well done sweetheart, you are doing great!".

When the celebration was over, our little girl accepted everyone's congratulations and was patiently waiting for her brother to come get her. The father of one of her friends had been there since the start of the celebration. He was hugging and kissing his daughter and encouraging her…"good job sweetheart, you were wonderful! Now, let's go home but first we will stop by the grocery store and the bakery to buy stuff for Christmas morning breakfast!". He lifted his daughter in his arms and they left. As he was lifting her in his arms, it seemed to our little girl that his hands were like big wide wings that held her tight and protected her. Her friend cuddled in her daddy's arms, calm, happy and with a big smile on her face.

She stands back, our little girl…from afar…in the kitchen…looking at her own father and wondering why when her father hugs her like that, she is not calm and happy and she is not smiling. Instead, she cries in terrible pain. And she is wondering why when this takes place no one is ever home.

Every time our little girl with the heavenly voice feels like that she runs to her brother and just grabs on from him. This is what she is going to do this Christmas, too.

A very different setting, right?

Why couldn't the kids of the second family be brother and sister with the kids of the first family and they too could dip their melomakarona in hot chocolate? Or why couldn't they be part of our childless teacher's family? And why must the indifferent and sick parents…be parents?

My Lord, You act in mysterious ways! I am hoping that You know something that we don't and that you pay back where necessary!

June 2010

June 29th 2010

*I*t has been a long time since my last entry. Many were the reasons! One reason was that this winter I travelled a lot for work, domestically and internationally. The main reason, though, was that I was becoming obsessed about the fact that Rena was not getting pregnant and I had started to fear that we are also on a road frequently travelled by other couples, friends of ours. So I did not want to write, I didn't feel like it; I would reinforce my obsession which I sort of knew was unreasonable.

Due to my travels, I didn't get together with my wife too often. I was away all the time and she was on duty all the time at the hospital. Our bed was usually empty as I was wandering from hotel to hotel and Rena kept spending her nights at the hospital, sleeping in a room signed "Staff – No Entry". Sometimes, the bed would be occupied, but by only one of the two of us. It was rare that both of us slept together in the big receptor of our love.

Why did I decide to dig out this file and start typing my thoughts on the white screen? Why do you think?

The good news is in! A little line on a pregnancy test informed us that in February we will be holding our own child in our arms! The moment that Rena announced the good news to me was hardly a "TV" moment, that is, during a romantic dinner or on the beach watching the sunset. I had just returned from the yard from feeding the chickens and walking the dogs, my clothes were dirty and I was dripping with sweat. Rena had just come out of the bathroom and she was in her cotton pajamas and had her hair wrapped in a towel

- "Yiannis…", she looked at me a little scared, like a little girl, and she waited before she blurred it out to give emphasis "…I am pregnant"
- "That is good news, my love" I replied quietly instead of actually doing what I wanted to which was to jump up and down and start yelling in relief. I kissed her and I could not even hug her, I was too dirty.

I asked her about the pregnancy test and she told me more details about the fact that it came out positive and so on and then we just stood there looking at each other with a sweet nervousness without knowing what to do next.

- Let me jump in the shower to get cleaned up and then we will go downstairs to tell your mom (her father was away those days to his yearly excursion to the monasteries of Mount Athos in Northern Greece).

Before I continue, however, let me go back in time to take things from the start.

Prompted by a business trip that I had to go on to Aspen in the US on June 16th, Rena and I decided that she would come with me and then we would make a stop at wonderful New York to spend some vacation time there. My first time in this magnificent metropolis was in February, again for business, and I was so flabbergasted that I told myself: "Rena has got to see this and experience it". It is completely opposite of our life in Samos that I was overly excited. I made a really good friend there in February, so we had someone to show us around the best of New York.

Before we left for Aspen, Rena was waiting for her period…she waited…and waited…but nothing. She also did a pregnancy test at the hospital but it came out negative. "Be cool Yiannis…" I told myself, "…it will come…at some point…", although I had a feeling that this time the baby would come. I don't know what it was that was telling me this inside me; maybe it was the incredible chemistry during the conception or maybe it was not even an intuition but just plain hope and desire.

Upon reaching Aspen, the symptoms started:

Symptom 1: Sleepiness

Rena likes her sleep; she takes after her father in that and her brother is the same, too. They are never late for work, but on the weekends and on holidays, they really like to sleep in. Even so, the way that Rena slept while we were in Aspen and New York was unprecedented. Endless hours of sleep were quite common during our stay there, especially in Aspen, where the altitude of around 2.500 meters forces even people like me, who due to advanced age need few hours of sleep, into a state of fatigue and sleepiness. With this symptom, I was faced with two challenges. What do I do while Rena is sleeping? The second one, which was the tougher of the two: how on earth do I wake her up?

- Baby, wanna start waking up?
- Mmmm...
- Darling, it is getting late, get up, we need to get to breakfast.
- Mmmm...

10 minutes later:

- Get up sleepyhead, we will be late.
- What time is it?
- Time to get up, baby.
- All right...5 more minutes...

As I was suspecting her state of pregnancy, I did not push her and I let her take her time

Symptom 2: Strange appetites

Before the pregnancy, if you wanted to be Rena's worst enemy, you would force her to eat boiled eggs. She couldn't even stand the smell of them. In Aspen, she ate two every morning. In fact, one of the mornings at breakfast, the boiled eggs were finished and I had to go into the kitchen of the hotel and ask them to bring out some more.

When her dish included asparagus, she would always pass them on to me and I was glad to receive them. In New York, she actually enjoyed eating them.

Melon was a fruit that she used to eat before she got pregnant but not with great enthusiasm. In New York, melon of all colours was the main ingredient in her fruit salads.

Her strong dislike of feta cheese and milk remained intact.

Symptom 3: Enhanced sense of smell

As we were walking along the busy streets of Manhattan or as we were shopping in the stores, Rena would suddenly stop doing whatever she was doing and would start sniffing the air trying to discover where some sort of intense and usually unpleasant smell was coming from. Pregnant women have enhanced sense of smell and taste. I couldn't share her feeling or confirm the intense smell and that reinforced my belief that she was pregnant. I would smile slyly and she'd get angry. She was suspecting her condition herself with all the above symptoms and with her period not coming but she was afraid to admit it. Perfectly understandable! I cannot even begin to imagine how a woman feels when she realizes that she will give life to a human being and that her body is going to undergo amazing changes in the following nine months.

So, the test is positive! It is time to tell the parents. They have the right to know first. Not because they are parents but because they are great parents!

– You are pregnant sweetheart?

Cries of joy and tears of happiness started coming out of my mother-in-law who could not stop hugging her daughter and her son-in-law.

My father-in-law was away to the holy grounds of the monasteries of Mount Athos. His cell phone had very bad reception and we couldn't get a hold of him easily. We talked about how much he would want to be home with us for the news but my mother-in-law thought that he would give a special meaning or symbolism to the fact that when he found out he happened to be in this sacred for him place.

Immediately after, I called my parents and they learned the good news, too. It was difficult for me to feel their happiness over the phone but I had to tell them right away. I guess I would have preferred to tell them in person instead of over the phone but it isn't possible. They live in the city of Korinthos which is close to Athens and far from Samos. What I did feel from them was sweet relief. They were also probably and secretly sharing my concerns and when they heard the news, they felt like their prayers had been answered. Surely a small thank-you donation will be made to their church. I wanted so much to be able to give them these news because they are older than my in-laws and I wished for them to have the joy of being grandparents from me, too. My brother already has two daughters.

June 30th, 2010

Today we did all the blood tests that were necessary to confirm the accuracy of the pregnancy test from the drugstore. Our little person is on its way and from the test results it is obvious that we will not have twins. Now it is time to announce the news to the brothers.

My brother, Antonis, is 5 years older than I am, so he is 40 going on to 41. He lives in Athens and he is working in one of the biggest and most luxurious hotels in Athens as night administrator for the closings of the bars and restaurants of the hotel. He is married and he has two daughters, Sia, who is in Junior High and Vassilikoula who is in kindergarten.

Antonis is a man who is well-built, not very talkative,

very reserved in what he says or does and extremely clever. When you first meet him, he gives you the impression that he is very tough and conservative. When you get to know him better, or rather, when he decides that it is time for you to get to know him better, you will see that he possesses a great sense of humor and that he cares and worries about the people around him. He has the unique ability to level any conversation in such a hilarious way that you cannot help holding your stomach from laughing. I am very proud of my brother because at difficult times he set his family as number one priority and together with his wife they have managed to hold it together and raise two wonderful children.

So how do I tell Adonis? I had to find a special way to impress them.

- Good evening, it's Yiannis.
- Hey Yiannis, what's up?
- All is well, how are you?
- We are fine, too. How is Rena?
- She is fine, here next to me. Can I talk to Sia?
- Sia? Sure…but why?…what's going on?
- Nothing is going on. I just want to talk to my niece.
- OK?…Sia…come to the phone, it's uncle Yiannis
- Hi Yiannis, how are you? How is Rena?
- Oh we are just fine. Sia, I have a question for you.
- Yeah, I am listening.
- Would you like to have a little cousin from Rena and me?
- Yeah…Definitely!!
- Well, you shall have it in February!

– Is Rena pregnant?
– Yes!
– Rena is pregnant…Rena is pregnant…!

It was red alert in my brother's house. Sia kept yelling repeatedly "Rena is pregnant", Vassilikoula was jumping up and down on the couch and my sister-in-law grabbed the phone from Sia's hands to congratulate us and talk with Rena…as mother to mother now!

It was intentional that I chose Sia to be the first member of my family's brother to learn about her new cousin. My niece was the first baby in the family, the first grandchild for my parents, my first niece for me. When Vassilikoula was born, Sia, instead of being jealous and causing trouble in the family, helped her mother a lot and welcomed the new baby from the very first moment she was brought home. By telling her first, I wanted to show her that she is an important part of this family and that I am glad that she will be the big cousin of my child. Of course, my kid will be closer to age with Vassilikoula but an older cousin is always good to have around to straighten out the little ones, when necessary.

Rena's brother, Makis, is 29 years old and also a doctor. He aims to be a psychiatrist. He is engaged to Fotini who is a teacher. Fortunately, Makis and Fotini met in Samos and she lives in Samos permanently which made Makis come live on the island, too. Besides relatives, we are all good friends, too. Makis has a lot of things in common with Adonis which is a little weird, the fact that our brothers are so much alike. He is very reserved and incredibly intelligent and he is also the kind of person that gives you the wrong first impression of who he really is. His tough and conservative exterior hides well his open-mindedness and sensitivity. He loves and respects his family greatly and anything that revolves around it. He is very protective of his sister and is a sleepless guardian of hers. He watches from a distance, as discretely as possible, if his sister gets along all right and I cannot but respect that.

I had to find a special way, too, to tell Makis that he is about to become an uncle. Coming home from work in the afternoon with Rena and my mother-in-law, who happened to be in the town of Vathi for errands, we were discussing the results of the blood test and that it is time for the brothers to find out.

- Yiannis, I will call Makis to tell him.
- Don't tell him over the phone, better in person.
- When and how do you think?
- Mmm…why don't we invite them over for lunch today?
- Yes, Good idea! I will cook for everyone! (that enthusiastic offer came from the back seat of the car from my mother-in-law who always makes sure to gather the family around the kitchen table once or twice a week)
- What if they are already invited at Fotini's mother?
- Then invite them over for coffee after lunch. Tell Makis that I want to talk to him. If you tell him that, he won't force you to tell him why we are inviting them because he will probably think "for Yiannis to want to talk to me, something is up".

They accepted the invitation and they came over for lunch. We managed to create an intriguing atmosphere, enough to make them wonder what is going on.

Some time ago, every time we met Makis and Fotini for coffee or drinks, he would ask us when we will make him an uncle, how much he wants a little niece or nephew and so on. In the beginning it was cute but because he wouldn't get an answer from us, he insisted. Of course, he couldn't realize that we were trying but hadn't reached the desired result yet, which is not easy to just talk about. His intentions were in the right place and he couldn't imagine that his sister and his brother-in-law could be facing some sort of problem in that area.

One day I told him: "And how can you be sure that we are not trying and for some reason we can't conceive, theoretically speaking, of course?" After that, he never asked again.

Before lunch, we were all sitting in the living room waiting for Rena to come downstairs so that we can tell them the news. Rena initiated:

- Makis, we called you here today because Yiannis wants to tell you something very important but before that, let me tell you that you should get ready to spend some money.
- Why?
- Tell him Yiannis!
- You were breathing down our necks all this time to make you an uncle, right? Well, you can start paying for some stuff for your niece or nephew as of February!

Makis' reaction was restrained and cool. He said with his deep voice that characterizes him and makes him sound like a little kid trying to talk as a grown-up:

- Really?

Fotini was not expecting it at all and at first she looked at us with an expression of puzzlement. As soon as it clicked in what was going on, she jumped from the couch like a spring. She yelled out "Sweetheart...!" and she ran towards Rena and hugged her so tight and with such honest joy that it was really touching to see. Something was different now when you looked at them hugging and being all excited.

It was as if you were looking at two little girls that were playing and one of them brought a Barbie doll to play with and share. This doll meant the world to them. The joy and significance of motherhood was expressed in the specific scene as the subconscious childhood dream of every woman to become a mother. I wonder how similar the two pictures would be. In the one picture you can see a mother receiving her newborn for the first time and in the other one you can see a little girl receiving her first doll. It is true that society prepares women from a young age to become mothers and be good at this sacred role. We teach them early which their destiny is or at least which their destiny could be as long as it is desired by them.

In this way stereotypes are created and often our society is accused for that. Can I ask something, though? Is that so bad? If you don't gradually prepare a little girl that at some point in the future she could be a mother, who will you prepare, a little boy? Is there an alternative? I am wondering if the social stereotypes for this specific issue are not at all guided by the need of society to cast all women in the same mould so that...blah...blah...blah...but are actually defined by nature. The instinct of survival and the need of the species to dominate lead us to multiply, to care for and protect our babies and, yes, to train little girls from a young age to become mothers. What more normal and natural than that?

What followed after we told them? Moments of family happiness and racket, lots of questions and discussions about the pregnancy, always accompanied by my moter-in-law's cooking. Makis seemed thoughtful and didn't say much until he blurred out the question that had been on his mind all this time:

> – What can you talk about with a baby? I mean, don't get me wrong, babies are nice but it gets on my nerves that you can't hold a conversation with them. And if you talk to them, do they understand or is it like talking to a wall?

Makis had already created images in his head. He was imagining him and the new baby playing or taking walks. Makis would talk to him or her and would do his best to explain the world around us and teach him/her the basics. He would love his sister's child so much that he would wonder in agony if what he explained was registered properly.

I mentioned before that the blood test showed that we don't have twins. Rena and I always thought about the possibility of having twins and if that would be something that we would welcome. I always got panicky thinking about it. Rena thought that she would kill two birds with one stone. I guess that having twins is something that you should not even start imagining what it is like because if you don't live it, you can have no idea. The emotions, the fatigue, the breakdown of the care, the expenses, the non-existent personal time…the double blessing!

Today we invited Maritsa over to tell her. Maritsa is my father-in-law's sister, that is, Rena's aunt. Besides that, she is also Rena's godmother, maiden of honor for my in-laws and for us, as well. Maritsa lost her husband a few years ago and has no children for personal reasons that will not be mentioned here and I am not really sure of. It doesn't matter, though; she has us, all of us. She is a very dear member of the family and that is why she has taken on so many different roles in it. She is a good listener and she likes discussing the current family issues and she is always willing to help in any way she can. You can talk to her about anything no matter how advanced it may be for her time. She has the ability to adjust quickly to the new times and to any emerging trends. Her work has probably contributed to that. She was in the film industry for many years, working as a make-up artist in many Greek films and series. She has worked with everyone; she has seen and heard everything.

– How was your trip, guys?
– Good Maritsa, it was really good. It will be our last, though, for a long time.
– It's all right, you've been on many trips, next time you can go again, you will.
– Well, it's not that we don't want to or we can't but that Rena mustn't go on so many trips anymore.
– Why?
– Because she can't be on the plane for many hours or go through the security check machines with the X-rays and everything.
– Why?
– Oh my Goodness Maritsa…cause pregnant women are not supposed to be exposed to X-rays.

A lot of screaming and crying and hugging took place after that, you know the drill. What is special here is that Maritsa's heart started racing and Rena had to intervene as a doctor, not only as a niece and godchild, to calm her down and make sure she does not need hospitalization. Maybe we should have come out with it a little easier, we almost sent het to her Creator much much earlier!

- Make sure you are OK cause we will need you to babysit for us!.
- Oh yes, of course, whatever you need!

July 2010

July 1ˢᵗ, 2010

Today we intended to start telling our friends but Maritsa ended up making it much easier for us. We told her in confidence and she confided in Rena's aunt, who is her cousin Maria's mother and Maritsa's sister. She told her daughter and Rena's best friend and while we were getting ready to go out for a coffee to get away from all the baby-mania, the cell phones started ringing like crazy. "Congratulations…" "We are so happy for you…", "It's gonna be a boy, I can feel it…", "Mark my words, you will have a girl…"; all these nice wishes started coming in, wishes that follow such beautiful moments. Maritsa was upset that the situation got out of control because that wasn't her intention. The truth is that I got a bit pissed off because I would have preferred to tell the people that found out in person and individually. It's all right, though! Maritsa really made things easier for us. After all, wishes and all this fuss for such happy events are more than welcomed. All is well then; our close friends and relatives are being informed.

July 3rd, 2010

Laskarina, as I mentioned before, is something like a sister to me. She should have been one of the first people that I would tell the news, the good news, but I was hesitant.

In December, she had her second artificial insemination. I was hesitant to tell her our news because she didn't get pregnant. I was hesitant to write about this since December because what has happened since then has shocked me in so many levels that it hurt too much to write. I couldn't manage my feelings well enough to put them on paper… or screen.

During the first fortnight of December the procedure was scheduled to take place. I knew the date and I called her to see how she is and encourage her a bit. As we always do in such cases, we started joking around after a while to lighten up the mood.

The results would come out on Friday. They did, but I found out on Monday. She called me while I was at work. I was certain that the results were negative since she didn't call me over the weekend.

     – Hello?
     – Hey Yiannis, it's Laskarina.

I froze…

     – Hey girl, what's up?
     – The results are in! Guess what? I am pregnant!

As I was holding the cell in my ear, I got up from my desk and went out of the building trying to articulate any words. Through my sobbing, I managed to say "Good stuff…Congratulations!"

- Come on, don't get so emotional, it's all right!
- Why didn't you call me over the weekend?
- There was a lot of fuss around here, you know. By the time we realized what was going on and tell the whole family, I didn't find time to calm down and call you.
- Tomorrow I am coming to Athens for a night, the day after I leave for Yiannena, and then I come back to Athens and then I leave again for Thessaloniki, for work again. Wanna meet up tomorrow?
- Absolutely, let's meet and catch up.
- Perfect, I will call you tomorrow to arrange.

On Tueday, we met in Athens in this great little bar in Gazi to talk over a glass of wine. Laskarina's face was unbelievably calm and her moves were confident and elegant. The relief was clearly shown on her face; she had gone through a lot of pain. You could tell that she felt blessed for the small miracle that was happening inside her.

I told her about my concerns that we hadn't conceived yet. She said it was still too early.

- It is still early to determine if there is a problem but because I know you well all these years, you'd better get that test you were talking about. You are the kind of person that needs to know now.
- Yes, you are right; I would rather know if indeed

there is a problem so I can start dealing with it now instead of waiting for a whole year to find out.

— If you were someone else, I would tell you not to do it so that you wouldn't put so much strain on yourself. But because you are a special case… you will get stressed if you don't know and live with the doubt, so do it.

— What exactly do I need to do?

— Oh, it's nothing, Marios has given sperm twice already. You will call the clinic, set up an appointment and go on the day and time they will tell you and you can carry out your… deposit.

— And…how does it all happen?

— Don't you know?

— That's not what I mean, smart ass…! I mean what is it like in there? What do you do exactly?

— They give you a little cup and you wait your turn to get inside the little room. It is quite funny watching all these guys waiting and holding their little cup.

— Oh yeah!…really funny Laskarina…!

— They all have the same nervous look on their face. In the room there are all sorts of aids like…

— Yeah yeah I get it…magazines and movies… what great fun!

I was so happy! I felt that justice on my friend had finally been served. I was looking at Laskarina and I could remember the teenage girl that I had met during that awkward age. She was a tomboy that loved to wear jeans, long-sleeved T-shirts and boots. Being more mature than her age, she was everyone's advisor. Us guys used to say amongst us: "Laskarina could be really hot if she dressed up". "That's right, and she's got a great face, she doesn't even need any makeup". Her Mediterranean features, long dark hair, big black eyes and full lips were well respected by the guys who did not really dare ask her out as her strong charming features matched her strong, dynamic and intimidating character.

This tomboy was sitting across from me now, a beautiful woman, glowing as a mother-to-be who will bring into this world a little person made by her and her husband.

The next day, on Wednesday, I left for Yiannena in Northern Greece, looking forward to returning to Athens as I was invited for dinner on Friday night by Laskarina and her husband to celebrate.

When I returned on Thursday, it was late afternoon. I had to dress up in a suit and attend a dinner in Kolonaki, downtown Athens. The dinner was held in a fancy restaurant in honor of some wineries. I reached the restaurant and I sat at my table waiting for two colleagues to show up. I had time to call Laskarina and arrange for the next day, I was anxious to see their new house, too.

- Hi there, how are you?
- Are you back? Didn't you get my text?
- No. When did you text me?
- Yesterday.
- I didn't get anything. There was really bad weather, maybe that's why. What's going on? I called to arrange for tomorrow.

I went numb when I heard her response.

> – I miscarried.

She started crying. I didn't know what to say. I usually do. You know what to say when you are prepared or when you have experienced something similar before. Many years ago a good friend wrote to me that his wife had miscarried but this time I was not prepared. Why the hell should I have been? Why? Of course, I wasn't! I had thought that their troubles were over. Obviously, I was very optimistic and could think of no wrong. Obviously, I had believed that God had finally set things straight after 3 years.

I don't care how disrespectful I am going to sound, but why God? Why can't You work your miracle this time? Don't give children to those who abuse them, those who beat them, those who scar them for life. Don't give them to those who give them life and then burry them in their gardens, to those who have them work for their daily bread, to those who promote them to prostitution. They are Your angels, Your creations which You send to us. How can You send them to those useless breeders? I can't say parents because such people are not parents. How can You force Your angels to live with them? How can You kill an angel? I don't understand…fuck I don't! I never will! Just wait! When my time comes and I get up there, we shall have a long chat, You and me, up close and personal.

Laskarina explained to me that her body apparently did not accept the baby and on Wednesday morning she miscarried.

And then came the second shock, during the same phone call. In the awkward and frozen silence, she said to me in a tone that hinted that she had forgotten to mention something.

– Oh…listen…don't tell Rena you are going to do the sperm test.
– Why not?
– You will make her nervous and there is no reason for that. When you come back to Athens, we will arrange it together. Don't tell her, I forgot to mention it the other day.
– OK…whatever you say.

Why was I shocked? Do you realize what had happened? I couldn't have a better friend in my life. In the midst of her desperation and pain for the lost embryo, she remembered to advise me. I wish that you all have such friends in your life.

Such people deserve to make and raise children!

July 5ᵗʰ, 2010

Today we came to Athens to see the doctor. Our gynecologist is my father-in-law's good friend. He has his office in Moschato, where we stay when we come to Athens, which is extremely convenient.

Our appointment was for 8 in the evening. We left his office at 9. God bless this good man! What a patient doctor! He explained and clarified so many things to us and when we left his office, our minds were at ease.

Well, fathers-to-be, listen to what the doctor had to say…I kept notes!

If your wife is a doctor, she can no longer do extra night shifts…no negotiations here…no way!

Her diet must be normal. She is not eating for two and she doesn't need to gain 30-40 pounds to say that she has a regular pregnancy. On the contrary, she must definitely have a good breakfast, a normal lunch and a light dinner consisting of some kind of protein like fish or chicken. Not too much fat, not too much sugar. The fetus cannot metabolize sugar like we do and most of it turns into fat. As the doctor said: "We do not want a big baby, we want a normal-sized baby which is going to be healthy and easy to get out.". Artificial sweeteners are forbidden, as are light sodas. Regular sodas are fine but scarcely as they contain a lot of sugar. In general, that's it, but please get the rest of the information from your doctor or dietician.

She must not lift, pull or push anything heavy.

She must not be locked up in a golden cage. She must keep on living as before. She can drive but only until a specific point in her pregnancy, the doctor said he will let us know.

She should exercise but the exercise must be very modest and not at all tiresome. Walking is a perfect way for her to move without the risk of pressuring her body and it is also a way to get out and enjoy an active social life.

If she smokes, 1-2 cigarettes a day are allowed. It would be better if she didn't smoke at all but if she has been smoking for years and she feels it is difficult for her to quit altogether, then she can have 1-2 smokes a day. Usually, as the pregnancy progresses, pregnant women reduce the amount of cigarettes they have on their own, without much effort. They tend to have a natural repulsion from it.

What surprised me the most was that the doctor told us that she could have one glass of wine or beer per day. I really couldn't believe it and I told the doctor that this came in contrast not only with everything I have heard till today but also with the content of seminars about wine that I have attended. Our teacher had told us that alcohol during pregnancy is strictly forbidden because it could cause problems. The doctor reassured me that "hard" liquor drinks with higher contents of alcohol are the ones strictly forbidden. Wine and beer are low in alcohol and do not affect the fetus as long as their consumption is limited to one glass per day. Although I completely trust our doctor, I am a bit skeptical, maybe because I don't have specialized knowledge. Anyway, I am glad that my Rena drinks very little in general and almost never "hard" liquor.

You can have sexual relations with your wife, at least at this early stage in the pregnancy. I had to ask the doctor to explain to me how the fetus is not affected by the act and he was very descriptive and clear. I suggest that you openly discuss it with your doctor without being embarrassed as there is no reason you should stop enjoying your love life.

She can swim in the sea as long as the water is not too cold and the waves are not too big. It is best to choose shallow beaches with calm, warm water. We did not ask about swimming pools because Rena avoids them anyway due to the susceptibility of women to pick up something not so nice from the pool water.

She must not sunbathe at all. She should always be in the shade of an umbrella.

It is advisable to avoid air travel due to the turbulence and the stress created during the flight. Also, she must not go through the X-ray security check due to the exposure. Just tell the airport employee that the lady is pregnant. They will have her go around the machine and they will do a physical body search. Today afternoon, as we were passing through the security check in the Samos airport, I leaned over and whispered to the airport employee that Rena is pregnant and she cannot go through the machine. I whispered in an effort to be as discrete as possible because there were a lot of people behind us in line and I didn't yet feel comfortable announcing it. The guy replied in the same discrete, almost conspirational tone of voice: "Oh…Ok sir… no problem!" , giving me the impression that he understood my need not to go public with this. So then he turns to his colleagues and does the exact opposite of what I was expecting him to do. "This lady is pregnant!", he shouted with honest enthusiasm and austere sense of duty. I think they must have heard him out on the runway. Rena and I looked at each other and laughed.

Last instructions: LOVE your wife or companion, take good care of her and protect her. She is carrying a piece of you inside her. The pregnant woman is sacred! She is the reason we continue existing. There should be a special day once a year devoted to the Holy Pregnant and She should be adored and worshipped with religious rituals as the other saints and holy people are. What goes on inside her is the most perfect thing that God and Mother Nature have created, a well set up, technically proficient process that creates the most superior being on planet Earth, the human being. Churches should be built for the Holy Pregnant in which She will be celebrated by Her faithful believers.

Be there for her, as much as you can! Live and experience the whole process with her! These are unique moments that you will regret missing. Don't distance yourself and think that this does not concern you. You will be a better father, if you experience everything that she is going through together and you will surely be a better husband. Arrange your work schedule in such a way that you are able to escort her to the doctor's appointments, to the ultrasound appointments, to the shopping for the baby, to the shopping for herself now that her body will be changing and she will need a lot of support. .

Pay attention to her and don't focus all your conversations on the baby. Show interest for her first and then the baby. I will tell you more about that later when we have acquired some sort of routine.

I guess you realize that this last set of instructions was not given to me by the doctor!

July 7th, 2010

There are some days in our life that define us or alter us or both. Today was one of those days for me. Today I witnessed the miracle of life right before my eyes. Today I felt like a father for the first time ever.

At 10 in the morning we had the first baby's ultrasound appointment in Pireas. We were on time, as always! We are always on time for all our appointments, it is almost obsessive! The doctor's assistant had us wait in the little lounge. We waited, both of us in nervousness and not knowing what to talk about. We looked through some books that were on the coffee table, mainly books with instructions for future parents; we commented on the cookies that were waiting to be consumed by the pregnant ladies. We observed this lady that came after us. She was quite thin and all you could see on her was a nice round tummy.

"How far along is she?" I wondered. "Why is she here alone?", "Where is her husband and if he couldn't come with her why didn't her mother or her mother-in-law? How can they leave her on her own at times like these? I wonder if her husband is not that involved or is too busy to take some time off to escort his wife to the ultrasound exam. Anyway, I shouldn't assume things and be so judgmental, who knows what her story is! I just wish everything is well with her pregnancy!"

Our first ultrasound in week 6! I had no idea what to expect.

The doctor cane out to the waiting area and called for Rena. We got up, we introduced ourselves and she told Rena to use the washroom before the exam.

– Yiannis, I am going to the washroom now, you wait at the lounge.
– What? Why? I want to be in the room with you.
– I know, but maybe the doctor will have a problem with it.
– I don't think so! All dads go in!

When she came out of the washroom, we waited a while and then the doctor came.

– Please, go ahead, let's start.
– Are you OK with me coming in, too, doctor?
– Of course!

Why didn't Rena want me inside?

The doctor showed Rena where to lie down after she took off her underwear. "But, if she is going to rub some gel on her tummy and rub it around with that gadget we see on TV, why did she ask her to take off her underwear? Oh, maybe she doesn't want to risk getting any gel on it by accident!", I thought. Rena laid back and while the doctor was preparing all the equipment they chatted, the two doctors together. "Where exactly do you work?", "Are you enjoying your internship?", etc.

While they were talking, the doctor grabbed a long tool, around 20cm long, rounded at the end, it looked a little like a small rolling pin. "That does not look like those things they show on TV. It must be something new. She is going to put the gel on my wife's belly and rub it around with that thing that looks like…you know what…", I thought. Somewhere between their conversation, "So, how are things at the hospital of Samos?", "Well, you know, a lot of running around, too many on-call shifts…", the doctor takes a condom as big as any man would wish that he was using and puts it over the "rolling pin" with the scandalous shape. At that exact moment I realized why Rena didn't want me to go inside with her. The exam would be intravaginal. She was afraid I wouldn't have the stomach for it.

    –   Ahh…doctor…is that where it will be done?
    –   Of course, at this early stage of the pregnancy the exam is intravaginal.
    –   Ohhh…right…I didn't know that…ok.

I was holding Rena's hand and she looked at me with a very calm look.

Suddenly, I heard a repetitive beat and I saw the doctor draw back in surprise. I was about to tell her that there is something wrong with the equipment (since I have such avid expert knowledge of the function of medical equipment…!) and that's when I realized that what I heard beating so loud was the heart of our child. I looked at the doctor in question and before I had the chance to ask her, she said: "Yes, it is the heart of the child! Rena, you are not 6 weeks in the term of pregnancy as you thought but you are about to close the 8th."

I cannot exactly describe how I felt, but I will try. The room was flooded by the sound of the heartbeat of our child. Rena listened in awe and surprise and the doctor was very pleased with the frequency and intensity of the beats. My eyes became all wet and I felt my body numb from happiness. Nothing else existed at that moment and nothing else mattered.

As I was turning my head left and right listening to this magical beat, I glanced at the screen and I saw this tiny little thing that had a very small body and four protrusions, like little wings, and a small head, all of the above in embryo size, of course.

    – Is that the baby?
    – Yes, it is!
    – Rena, look!
    – I am!

Through its little body and between the two extremities that are going to be its hands, you could see its heart beating, fast, strong…lively!

It was incredible! Our child! I was standing there in utter awe. I had just experienced the most beautiful miracle. I felt so very blessed. In 5 minutes I had changed. I was not the same Yiannis as I was when I entered the doctor's office 20 minutes before. The exam room door had opened, I had walked in as Yiannis and I walked out as Yiannis-father-to-be. Good thing I insisted on going in the room, too.

    – Its beats are 155 per minute. It seems to be a
      very strong baby. Congratulations!

After we thanked the doctor and arranged the next appointment for August 11th, we took the envelope with the picture of our baby and all the medical parameters and we went on our way. We immediately started calling everyone who was waiting to find out what happened, parents, brothers, friends, describing our experience in as much detail as possible. I was holding the envelope under my armpit tightly and I felt a sense of protectiveness coming over me. In this envelope was my child, I will never let anyone touch it and get it dirty!

    – Rena, let's go for a coffee at the square before

we go on. I feel like I need to sit down and regroup.

My eyes were still dripping.
We sat down and kept looking at its picture.

–   Our baby is strong, right Rena?
–   Yes, that's what the doctor said; its heartbeats are very good!
–   Unbelievable experience!
–   Really!
–   I am glad I didn't listen to you and came inside with you.
–   I thought you might feel weird because the exam was intravaginal.
–   I can't say that I was too thrilled when I saw that…thing…directed towards you!

As we were talking a sweepstake salesperson walked by and asked us if we felt lucky and we thought…"Why not? You never know! It is a special day today!"

–   How much is the whole set?
–   10 euros.
–   There you go…and, by the way, here, take a look at the picture of our baby, we just did the first ultrasound. Here it is…there is its little heart, too…it beat so loudly!
–   Wow, congratulations! May it live long and be healthy!
–   Thank you very much! We wish the same for you!

I guess my insanity had just begun.

July 8th, 2010

Last night, we invited the "gang" over the house in Moschato. Almost all of us were there. The 4 girlfriends with their husbands, only Maria's boyfriend couldn't make it. Obviously, I showed everyone the picture of the baby and, of course, they were all enjoying my enthusiasm and the expression of satisfaction that was written all over my face.

After we shot the breeze for a while, the next topic on the agenda was the upcoming birth of Loukia's and Stamati's child. Loukia was almost due and she had a really round belly. She was calm and she was in sweet anticipation of the time her doctor would tell her to go to the maternity clinic or when her water would break. Her doctor was a bit concerned about the placenta as it was aging too fast and he had warned Loukia that he may notify her to go in at any given moment.

We had arranged to return to Samos with the next day's flight. Rena complained to Loukia.

– Girlfriend, it's a pity that you didn't go into labor these days that we have been here...I would love to be here to see the little guy!
– Who knows? It could be tonight!
– Oh I wish! If it is, call us immediately so we can be there!
– That goes without saying! Well, for now, let me call the doctor and see what he tells me.

Loukia left the kitchen and went out to the balcony to talk to the doctor in private. I assume you have already figured that we were again sitting in our natural habitat, which is the kitchen, where a grand feast was in progress from leftover home-cooked food that my mother had brought, Chinese food and souvlaki take-out. My parents, who had already visited us, had brought over a lot of plastic containers with home-made delicacies.

Out on the balcony, Loukia was arranging something with her doctor in a very professional manner, as if she was arranging a meeting for the next day or closing a serious deal. When she came back inside, she announced that what she was arranging with her gynecologist was to go in the hospital the next morning at 8 am…for labor! We were all so excited and after giving all our attention to Loukia, we turned to Stamatis who was smiling trying to reply to us asking him: "How do you feel about becoming a father tomorrow?" How can one answer that question? How can you even know what you are feeling? You can only approximate your emotions.

So, today, the first thing I did as soon as I woke up was to call Olympic Airlines and change our tickets for Friday morning instead of this afternoon. Fortunately, I found seats. We were all set to go to the maternity clinic to stand by our friends, to become witnesses to their most personal moments and to welcome little Panos in our lives.

While we were getting ready, Rena sat on the edge of the bed, looking very thoughtful and slightly scared. She turned and looked at me:

- What's wrong honey?
- Yiannis, I don't know if I want to go to the hospital.
- Why is that?
- I am not sure, I think I am scared.
- But your girlfriend is about to have a baby, you don't want to miss that!

– No, you are right, I don't, but I don't want to walk in there.
– Are you afraid of seeing what we are going to go through in a few months?
– Yes.
– All the more reason to go, so you won't develop some sort of phobia.

I really didn't need to convince her much, one of her best friends was in labor, she wouldn't miss it for the world.

When we reached the maternity ward, Rena and Maria and myself, the soon-to-be grandparents and Olga, the anxious sister, were all there waiting at the lounge. Stamatis was inside with Loukia in one of the delivery rooms. Loukia's father seemed to be lost in space. When you looked at him, you could almost see Loukia's life flashing before his eyes. If I could put his agony into words, I think he would say: "My little girl! It feels like yesterday that I held her in my hands for the first time, such a tiny little creature with her hands trembling and looking up at me seeking for protection. And today, she is about to have hew own child, to give birth! Oh God, let it all go well and give her an easy labor!"

Loukia's in-laws were sitting in the lounge very quiet and apparently nervous. Her mother was trying to distract everyone and herself obviously, by making chit-chat; Loukia's sister would jump from her seat every time the doors of the delivery rooms opened and a nurse would call out relatives' names.

The atmosphere in the relatives' lounge was tense in an electrifying and happy way. Dads, grandmothers, grandfathers, aunts and uncles were waiting to hear the good news. Everyone was celebrating everyone else's happiness, they exchanged congratulatory hugs and handshakes and friends kept coming in with gifts and balloons. There was a constant flow of people in the room, coming and going. Those who came, expected to welcome a new baby in their lives and those who left changed floors, they went to the top floors of the building where the new mothers were taken to after their painful but extraordinary experience. My Rena sat and observed all this commotion happening around her and she seemed quite relieved and joyful. Relieved because she was there to stand by her friend and experience the whole thing and joyful because she was imagining her own family and relatives waiting for her when her time for the happy event comes. "I wonder how my father will react when he will wait in the lounge for me", she whispered to me.

Around noon, Stamatis came out and told us that the baby is not progressing and that the doctor does not want to risk waiting any longer. Panos was a stubborn little fellow but the placenta was no longer safe for him and he had to pop out.

– We have to have a caesarian section. The doctor doesn't feel comfortable waiting longer.

It wasn't the best news. Loukia had had the most normal pregnancy a woman could have so no one expected this turn of events. No matter how you look at it, a caesarian section is a surgical procedure and it does sound a bit scary.

Both sets of parents froze and sat down speechless. I couldn't deal with them at all and try to guess their thoughts because someone had to deal with Stamatis. I asked him if I should get him something to eat because he hadn't had anything since the morning. He declined; his stomach was tied up in knots.

– You know Stamatis, the advantage of the

caesarian is that the baby will not have a hard time coming out at all.

– You think?

– Yeah, the baby is not pushed though the regular route and, as a result, its face and little head don't get squished.

– Right, I've heard about that.

– Yeah, don't' worry everything is going to be fine. And don't worry about Loukia either, the procedure is really quick and easy. It's not how it used to be when they did a huge cut and left a big scar. You will see, the doctor will come out in a bit and will announce that all went well.

In order to distract everyone from the endless, tormenting moments of waiting, I asked Stamatis if he had brought a video camera with him. He had completely forgotten that he had indeed brought it along. He gave it to me and after he showed me how to use it, I started going around asking everyone to send their wishes to Loukia, on camera. As the moments went by and as my director's abilities were being put to the test, the nurse's voice was heard.

– Mr….?

She gathered us all in a special little room in which the comings of the newborns are announced to the relatives in private. That is exactly what she did. Both Loukia and the baby were fine! She asked us to wait and after a while she brought little Panos in the transparent plastic container so we could see him for the first time, so that his father could see him for the first time.

Stamatis leaned over him and touched his tiny hand and spelled out some words of love which I wouldn't document even if I had heard. Such moments are so sacredly personal that I consider it very intrusive for others to be around while they take place.

What a relief! Everything went well! Thank God! That evening we visited the happy mommy who was serene and smiling. Her room was full of balloons and gifts. The parents and the closest relatives brought sweets to treat the visitors; the room was full of boxes with ribbons containing sweet delicacies. .

These are small and big moments that seal parts of our lives. Panos, we greet you and welcome you in our world and we thank you for having the honor of being witnesses to your birth and your first day on this planet. You still haven't realized how lucky you are that you were born in this family…Yiannis and Rena are waiting for you at the island!

July 15ʰ, 2010   Week 9

Have you ever heard of horror stories of relatives fighting about the name of the child? Do you have any idea how many daughters-in-law are no longer in speaking terms with their mothers-in-law or how many sons got into arguments with their families about this, at least here in Greece? What is worse, so many grandmas and grandpas have terrorized the parents by telling them "when we were scared that the baby may not be healthy we promised St. This or That that we would give him His name if he was born healthy" or "Holy Mary came to my sleep last night and asked me to give the baby her name". The above are underhand tactics that psychologically blackmail the couple and have them wonder if they are telling the truth or not. But most couples don't risk it; they do not want to mess with the divine.

Rena and I had decided some time ago of what the name

of the child is going to be. Firstly, we had agreed that we will follow the custom of naming the baby after one of their grandparents. We don't feel we have to and it doesn't bother us plus it is nice to pay tribute in this way to the person that raised you.

If it is a boy, we will call him Antonis, after my father. My brother has two daughters and they most likely won't have any more kids. My father is the eldest of the two sets of parents and I would like for him to hear his name. If it is a girl, we will name her Thomais, after my mother-in-law, and we will call her Thomae or Thome. My mother, her name is Vasso, has heard her name from one of my brother's daughters. My mother-in-law will help us a lot with the baby since we are all staying in the same house temporarily. It will be fun to call out Thome and have two heads turn.

I called my parents today to inform them of the decision that we made. The reaction was very positive. My mother was certain that we would work it out in our heads the way we did, she thought the same way, too. My in-laws agreed, too. So, we will not have any unpleasant situations or any tragic inter-family quarrelling. That is fortunate because I would not want to deal with it. To be fair, though, none of our parents would bother with such issues as other parents might have, they wouldn't have minded whatever our decision would have been.

Some advice for couples: Do whatever you want! If your parents don't agree with the name that you want to give your child, then just give it the name that you had thought of originally and do not negotiate, do not even bother talking about it. Choose names that have nothing to do with any members of the family. This way, no one will feel left out as no one will be privileged. However, if a parent is so persistent in the child being named after him or her and even offers some sort of bribe in the form of writing over to the kid some piece of real estate or depositing a worthy to mention amount in a bank account for the new member, then it is best to give in! Who can resist a three-bedroom apartment or 25.000 euros in the bank, especially at times like these? Not to worry, when your child grows up and has his/her own home or a hearty bank account, he/she is not going to blame you for succumbing to materialism: " Why wouldn't you accept a gift from grandpa? What's in a name? Big deal!"

I told Rena I called them so that she knows:

– Why did you tell them so early?
– What do you mean?
– Didn't you want to wait till we find out the sex of the baby?
– I thought of that, but if it's a girl, my father won't have the sweet anticipation. I wanted him to know of our intentions cause I am sure that would make him feel honored and happy.

July 20*th*, 2010

It is July 20*th* today and our baby already has two presents waiting for it.

Maritsa came over a few days ago and told us that she had something to give us:

– I know it is still too early but I wanted to get something for the little one!

She gave us a huge bag which had a very soft, beige, stuffed doggy. It is as big as a 2-year-old child, it is lying on its stomach and it is very soft. It will be perfect for the kid's play area when it is a bit older. Surely he or she will hug it and fall asleep with it in its little arms. Thank you Maritsa!

The second present, which we received today, came from a good colleague at work. She went on holiday to the island of Tinos, the island visited by many Christians due to the grand church of Holy Mary and its miracle-performing icon. She was shopping around in one of the stores and she saw a little icon of Holy Mary. It is rectangular with a linen trim. "The minute I saw it, I thought of you guys and I bought it in case you want to hang it up in its room", she said to me with slightly shiny eyes. It is nice to know that there are people that already love our unborn, especially people like her and her husband. They have been tested many times and they are family-oriented Christians who deserve life's best. Thank you guys…thanks a lot!

July 24ᵗʰ 2010

The house we are staying in right now is small. It is above my in-laws' house, it has one bedroom, a living room, a small bathroom and a tiny kitchen. In a piece of land right next to my in-laws' house we are building our own three-story house, too big for our financial situation, which is progressing very slowly because of its size and the expenses necessary to complete. Our present little home, though, has a fantastic view and it has been cozy for us, so far.

Now with the baby coming, however, we need to get organized and regroup. Firstly, we will let him or her have our bedroom and we will turn the living room into a bedroom for us. Also, we need to create more room in the kitchen for all the gadgets that are necessary for the baby's care like boilers, sterilizers etc. We must start imagining how all the furniture of the baby's room are going to be set up, the cot, the baby changer, but also in our own room to make sure we are comfortable. So, the project "Sorting out" or "Nest's Syndrome" as Rena calls it is being put into effect.

The other alternative is to separate the living room in two rudimentary rooms, a smaller living room and a nursery. This way, we get to keep our room and not lose the functionality of a living room.

I think both of us want everything to be perfect, or as perfect as possible, for when our little one comes home. It is surely psychological, what we are feeling, because the baby won't be able to tell whether the rooms are tidy and organized or not. However, it can sense our emotional state. If everything is in its right place and we are able to move around the house with ease, we will feel good and we will be able to cope better with the staying up all night and the panic that is caused by the lack of experience when a tiny person comes home from the hospital.

25/07/10

We are in the 10th week and my Rena keeps feeling a bit sick to her stomach but without having any actual vomiting. She is very careful with her diet with only very limited "violations" and deviations from the doctor's orders. The hormones are having a blast inside her making Rena a bit more edgy. I am edgy, too, without any increasing or playing hormones and that is worse. I am not sure why but I have so many things to think about, so many chores and preparations. I can not focus on what is making me nervous and anxious but the thoughts and fears that keep passing through my small brain are many.

As far as our love life is concerned, it is not even an issue at this point. It is completely normal as Rena is experiencing physical and emotional fluctuations all day long and I see her as very fragile and vulnerable and I feel that she is going to "break" if I touch her in that way. I always thought that it would be weird and not such a turn-on for a husband to see his wife's belly change shapes. Actually, it does not bother me at all! She is so cute with her little tummy filling out slowly, week by week, and because she is careful with her diet, if you see her on the street walking from behind, you can not tell she is pregnant. Then, she turns around and there it is! Of course, it is still too early. Anyway, to me, that little tummy sticking out gives her an extra breeze of femininity. She thinks she is fat and she looks at me doubtfully when I tell her: "You are gorgeous! You are the most beautiful pregnant woman I have ever seen with the sexiest tummy ever!"

Coming back to her diet, Rena has stopped drinking alcohol not only because the doctor doesn't allow it but she herself does not feel like it anymore. Maybe it is some sort of defense mechanism or maybe it's just the small or big changes in taste that pregnant women have. What impressed me the most is that she doesn't like beef anymore. It smells funny to her. This is very odd considering that up till now there was no better meal for us than a juicy piece of bon-fillet cooked medium-rare-plus for Rena and medium-rare-minus for me accompanied by a carefully selected bottle of red wine. Even odder is her repulsion for ice-cream. Rena likes sweets so much that I would have never thought that she would experience any changes in her likings for sweet stuff. When I want some ice-cream, I have to go to a different room because she can't stand the smell of it.

When it comes to food, my mother-in-law's reactions are quite entertaining. During the first days after she found out we were with child she cooked for us every day recognizing how vulnerable a pregnant woman is in the beginning of the pregnancy. Seeing that I had taken over all the house cleaning chores and thinking that cooking would be extra work for me, she offered to cook for us every single day. Of course, that couldn't go on because I can cook myself and so can Rena as long as she doesn't lift heavy pots and pans. Adding to that, my mother-in-law has medical issues with her wrists, she had to undergo surgery to correct the problem and not hurt so much anymore. So I told her to cool down and not exhaust herself for us now because we are going to need her to be healthy and strong for when the baby comes along. How is she going to hold it, how is she going to pamper it, and most importantly how is she going to show us how to clean it after it poops?

The funniest of all is when she cooked something at night she would call us from the bottom of the stairs to pick up little plates of whatever she had prepared.

– But I am not hungry mom, I will not eat it.
– That's OK, just put it in the fridge and if you have a craving later, you can have it.

As a result, during the first month, when you opened our fridge you would find everywhere little plates of delicacies such as meat omelets, pancakes, etc. Most of those were consumed by Lulu, our dog, not because they were not good but because we are used to eating a bit lighter in the later evening.

When it comes to my father-in-law, Paraskevas, the most zany thing he has said and is very characteristic of his temperament was said during a family lunch that we were having. The rest of us were talking and he had drifted and was staring in the thin air. Then, he looked at us slyly and with an expression on his face that he is about to say something, he said:

> — You wait and see, this little one is going to get me to make a slide from the one terrace to the next!

Our house is built on the mountain on two terraces, two big steps you could call them. To get from the one part to the other you need to go down a stone-built staircase. My father-in-law has a vivid imagination and he could easily be a writer of children's books. He has the ability to take an object or an animal and build a little story around it, a story made to be read to children. So I am certain that as he was eating he was imagining himself out in the yard with his grandkid playing or with his grandkid watching him do the yard chores that he likes so much. He probably thought to himself how cool and naughty it would be to build a big slide leading from the top terrace to the bottom one. But this scenario would be too simple. He preferred to imagine it differently. It would be his grandkid's idea and it would go like something like this:

> — Grandpa, can you build me a big slide so I can slide from top to bottom, you know, like one of those slides that are at the playground you take me to?
> — A slide? Mmm, that is not a bad idea but I don't think grandma will care much for it since we will have to ruin part of her garden.
> — Oh, come on grandpa, please, it will be so much fun!
> — Well, we can think about it…if it is possible… how could we…?
> — Come on, I will help you!
> — All right, let me talk it over with grandma. We

> must find a way to convince her, you talk to her,
> too…you know!

It is obvious whose idea it would have really been and who would have had to convince who to do it! Sometimes, it is moving to see how my father-in-law combines the two different parts of himself, the serious, austere doctor and family man with an endless tenderness and child-like behavior that comes out of him unexpectedly and catches us all off guard..

We are coming to the end of the 3rd month and, as I mentioned above, there is some tension. Minor quarreling is not absent although we do try to avoid it. It is not good to create tension in an environment where a pregnant woman lives and functions. But, sometimes, it is inevitable. Rena, due to the increase of the hormones and the little factory that has been set up inside her with the aim of making our own little human being, has become more sensitive and little things that didn't use to bother her, now they do. For all the grumbling, the receptor is me. But who else could it have been? We usually take it out on the people who love us and live with us on a daily basis; consequently, they don't hold a grudge. As to me, I feel a heavy burden of responsibility on my shoulders, a burden that I have created myself and essentially it may not be that bad, that heavy. I must be strong, supportive, organized and all those adjectives that you must be in order to cope as a proper family man, husband and as a future father. I will be all those things, what else can I do? I want to be the man who takes care of his family. Nevertheless, sometimes I break down myself, too, and I react. If you throw into the equation the house chores that are all now my responsibility to do, then I guess it is understandable for me to get edgy now and then.

House chores, let's talk about that! I hope that none

of you reading this diary, especially the about-to-be dads, think that the mother of your child will be able to continue doing any house chores as she did before. If you didn't help her before which you should have anyway, now you will. Be proud that you are going to do the dishes, iron your and her clothes, vacuum and clean the bathroom because your lady can not be exposed to any of those chemical cleaning products. Be proud that you are going to get up on that ladder and clean the glass windows and that, generally, you will choose to do all those chores that require weight lifting or pulling or pushing. Gentlemen, our manhood is not defined by whether you do the above or not. Firstly, grand proof of your manhood is the son or daughter that is growing in the belly of your beloved and, secondly, a man must be a gentleman who respects and understands the psychosomatic condition of his companion and realizes that the wrong move or excessive tiredness can cause severe problems in a pregnancy.

If you can't do the house chores or don't want to or don't have the time, then you should hire someone once a week to do all the "heavy" and time-consuming ones and you can continue doing all the small, short things that are necessary to be done daily in order to maintain a clean and tidy home. If you can't afford it, then you could try to recruit your parents or your in-laws or your lady's close friends. In case none of the above is possible, then schedule your life in such a way that you find time to do them.

If you are not pregnant yet and you are not willing to do any of the above in the future, then things just got much simpler for you and for the woman who was "lucky" enough to choose you as the father of her child and for your child who will have a non-participating father. The solution is plain and simple. Don't reproduce. After all, such genes are not meant to be transferred to the next generation.

July 29th, 2010

Today is the first day that I have spoken to Laskarina after I told her our good news. I had a question for her in regards with her work, she is a journalist, so I called her on her cell in the morning. Marios picked it up and told me that they are on vacation in Creta island and that they are having a great time. An hour later, Laskarina called me back. She sounded very well on the phone, happy and cheerful, as she is most of the time.

Ever since I told her we are expecting, I was a bit worried of how she is going to take it, watching one of her best friends having a child when they had been trying for 3 years. I was so wrong, though, and I know she will be mad at me when she reads these lines one day. She is a true friend and she wouldn't feel anything else but joy for us regardless of her own drama. I am really sorry, Laskarina, for thinking even for one moment that you would feel anything negative for us. You have never done so and I know you never will!

August 2010

August 10th, 2010   Week 13

Tomorrow we are flying to Athens to have one of the most important ultrasound exams, the second one. With this one we want to measure "the nuchal translucency region under the skin behind the baby's neck". My own personal doctor and mother of my child explained to me that this screening test will show us if all its members are developing normally and will indicate the chances of the baby being born with Down syndrome or something similar.

Naturally, we are hoping that all is well and that we hear good news from the doctor. The anxiousness, though, is there, especially when you have knowledge, as Rena does. Those of us who are not doctors can not be aware of the details, the chances and the significance of some medical tests; therefore, we may not worry as much. I, for example, think that we are going to Athens to see our unborn child, like a visit, as if we have sent it to summer camp and this is a pre-arranged visit at the camp. Rena, on the other hand, is having nightmares that the baby is not healthy

The best-case scenario is that the fetus is as healthy as can be and that the pregnancy is continued, as scheduled. The worst-case scenario is that it has some sort of physical abnormality or will have some mental challenge and we will be forced to interrupt the pregnancy. I get weak in the knees just thinking of the second case. I am taking it out of my head, I don't even want to imagine it or prepare myself psychologically for that possibility.

August 11ᵗʰ, 2010

Today we had the second ultrasound exam. We sat at the doctor's lounge observing the other couples and all the pregnant women all waiting in agony. This time I saw many fathers there escorting and supporting the mothers-to-be. Maybe, due to summer time off, they had time to join them. It was a wonderful setting, seeing all these couples, strangers among strangers but all having something so important in common. And as I was watching the expressions on their faces and wondering what was going through their heads, a couple storms out of the examination room, both holding their cells on their ears and telling their parents, "It's a boy, it's a boy!".

One of the soon-to-be fathers was twirling a line of beads around his fingers and waited anxiously until the doctor called them. Another one was sitting calmly next to his wife holding her hand and just anticipating. Another one was more nervous and walked up and down the lounge unable to sit down and be patient. And another one, trying to get that awful second scenario out of his head, was observing the rest of them to pass the time and collect material for his diary.

Rena's agony was clearly evident on her face. Her expression today reminded me of her expression when she is flying during take-off and landing. She is afraid of airplanes and her worst moments on the plane are those two. She can't even talk during that time, she is dedicated to her fear and she lives every moment of it. That's how she was today.

We entered the room and the exam started, not intravaginally this time, fortunately! The doctor put gel on Rena's stomach, did all the measurements and moved around the probe to see the baby from all the sides. We saw its little hands and feet, its head, its nose and its heart beating. During the exam the doctor didn't speak, she just mumbled some Mmm's and "Aha's and "That's good!" and so on. Rena was hanging from the doctor's lips waiting for her to say anything definitely positive. At this point I started worrying and cold sweat was covering me because the exam lasted longer than I thought and the doctor was worryingly silent. The poor woman was just doing her job; it was us who were impatient to find out the results.

I think that today, right there in the examination room, we felt worry about our child, as parents do. It was the first time we felt that distress our parents had about us when we were sick or when we were away from home for some reason. But it came out so naturally, like an instinct and as if we were prepared for it. It was almost as if we were drawing the power to cope from within us but not from where we usually do. This was another source of power inside of us, one that is reserved only for the case that one becomes a parent, an extra source to draw from.

> – All right, we are done, congratulations, your little one is most healthy!

What a relief! She explained to us that all its members are developing normally, its little heart is strong and that the chances that it is mentally challenged in any way are so slim that they are practically non-existent. They took blood from Rena to confirm it. They will give us the results in 2 to 3 days.

So, it's all good, thank the Lord!

— What about the sex doctor, can't we see what it is?
— Ah, yes, just a minute, let's take a look!

The doctor had forgotten to ask us if we wanted to find out what it is. She tried her best to see if we would be buying cars or dollies but our baby would not open up its legs to give us a clear view. She squeezed here, she squeezed there, but nothing. I could see the baby getting squished through the inner walls of the sack and the doctor pushing it from the one side to the other and I felt like my child was being unnecessarily harassed. I wanted to see what my baby was going to be more than anything but it was not having fun getting "tossed" from one side of the sack to the other. I touched the doctor's hand very gently and lightly.

— We can't see it, can we, doctor?
— No, unfortunately not, the little stubborn one is not letting us, I always have this problem with colleagues' babies.
— Then, it's all right, just leave it, don't squish it anymore, please. We will find out next time.

Was that a bit overprotective on my part? Was that the first indication of my over-protectiveness?

That night, when we returned home after an evening

69

outing in the city, as we were waiting for the elevator, we talked about how everything went very well and how beautifully our day was ending. Rena said to me:

– It's a good thing everything went OK! When she was examining me I was so anxious that there were actually a few moments that I had stopped breathing.

I kissed her above her eyes, above her beautiful eyes, I hugged her and we walked into the elevator without saying another word to each other.

August 8th, 2010

Today's free day in Athens presented a great opportunity for shopping and meeting with friends. We had already arranged to see Laskarina and we met at Gazi, a really hip area in Athens. We met in one of my favorite restaurants for dinner.

We arrived first and after a while she showed up. She gave Rena a really big and tight hug and kept telling us how happy she is to see us and how excited she is about our news. She hugged me, too, tight and long, as always, and she joined us.

We talked, we dined, we laughed! Towards the end of the meal she told us that they are going to have another artificial insemination, most likely in January. They need to save up first. She is going to change doctors for psychological reasons. She is not thinking about adoption yet because in Greece the procedure can wear you down as it is very strict and lengthy. This is another sore spot of Greek society and I have not looked into it at all and due to it being a very serious issue, I will not touch upon it now. If only one day

I had the time, the energy and the access to look into it more deeply!.

My Rena, having a great perception of things, said to me on our way home:

– My feeling is that this time the procedure will be successful and her body won't reject the embryo. The change in doctor will help her psychologically. Besides that, she has extensive experience now and she will know exactly what she has to do.

I wish! I wish that the day Rena goes into labor Laskarina and Marios will be outside in the waiting room with their own munchkin conceived.

August 13ᵗʰ, 2010

Before we left for Samos, we had to visit Loukia and Stamatis. We wanted to check up on them and their new baby.

We visited them early in the afternoon. They didn't look as tired as I thought they would a month after the birth of their little Panos. They talked to us about the panic of the first days, the feedings, the changings, how much their parents have helped. The worst for them is the lack of sleep and personal time. Stamatis said to me:

– We are unable to plan anything right now. There can be no schedule, everything is always in the air and is determined by when the baby will wake up and sleep.

I have to confess, that was scary! The first days that we

will have the baby at home imagine very difficult to me. We will be such inexperienced parents, we will have no idea where to begin and end. I guess that in the previous expression only the first part applies, "where to begin". Once you have a child, there is no "end". I am not worried, though! We will find the power from that unexplored source that I mentioned before, from which you can draw courage only when you become a parent. I will name it the Babysource.

The Babysource will supply us with secret powers, superhuman, physical and mental. The Babysource will give us patience to bear with the non-stop crying and the seemingly inexcusable nagging of the baby. That is where we will find the love that is as important for the baby as is its milk. It will help us get up in the middle of the night to feed and clean the baby. Without the Babysource we won't be able to go to work and perform our daily duties trying to separate our personal from our professional life. Really, how can you attend a sales meeting with your full attention when there is a little angel waiting for you at home?

And will the Babysource be inexhaustible? Of course not! There will be times that it will have nothing to give. The only way for it to recharge is the baby itself and its reactions. When the baby is clean and fed and calm, then the Babysource will load up again. The love and patience that the parents take from it whenever they need it will be automatically returned when their little baby will look them in the eyes as if it would say: "Thank you! Thank you for taking care of me and loving me! I know it is a bit hard looking after me all the time in the beginning but please be patient. In a little while I will be able to talk and tell you what I want and need, we will play together, I will smile at you, I will hug you…a little more patience…!"

August 15ᵗʰ, 2010

August 15ᵗʰ for Orthodox Christians is an important religious day as it is the date of the passing of Holy Mary. The thoughts in my poor brain have less to do with the religious meaning of this day and more with the relationship between mother and son.   Passing through my head are all those images from the life of Christ and His Mother, images embedded in us at school, by the Scriptures, during those long chats with Grandma and by the religious films we watch on TV.

All the above were swirling in my head like instant movie shots when they all stopped at one memory, at the stunning view of the statue of Holy Mother and Jesus at St. Peter's Cathedral at the Vatican.

Last year, Rena and I left for a 3-day getaway to Rome. We had a perfect time; we always have a perfect time when we take a holiday. We, of course, visited the Vatican. Entering St. Peter's Cathedral, the Basilica, we were initially impressed by the size of the church. Moving along to the right there was in front of us one of the most expressive masterpieces that I have ever seen, Michelangelo's Pieta, an exquisite marble statue depicting Jesus laying back in the hands of His Mother after the crucifixion.

Jesus had been crucified and now, with his spirit surrendered to his Holy Father, has been taken off the cross. Holy Mary, always there for her son, is experiencing the most tragic moment of her life. She is sitting and on her lap they have placed her son. Jesus is surrendered in her arms with no life left in him any more. He is finishing the course of his life exactly where he started it, in the arms of his mother. She, a sad figure, is holding him and her eyes look down and she seems numb. She cannot cry any longer, there are no more tears left. Maybe she is relieved that her son's horrible ordeal is finally over. The co-existence of majestic sadness and dignity on her face as well as the complete surrender of her son's body on her lap make this work of art unique. And although it depicts death, it is strangely dynamic and alive with all the grief jumping out at you and leaving you breathless. Even though this is a sculpture depicting two grand religious symbols of the world, it is at the same time just an image of a mother who has just lost her child, the image of any mother. Surely at that time Mary was not thinking of the premature death of a religious and spiritual leader that was destined to change the world's history, she was not thinking that her son sacrificed himself for the good of humanity, instead she thought of the first hours when her baby was born. She remembered the first time they brought her son and laid him gently on her and the little one, after the traumatic experience of his birth, was relieved when he caught the smell of his mother. She remembered the first time he said "mama", his first steps, his toys…And now they bring him back to her…but how!

In some cases, cycles need to complete. But no parent should have to see their child's life cycle completed.

August 17th, 2010

Lately, I have had the pleasure of constantly replying to my wife to the question if I love her. Generally, we are a gushy couple and we talk about our feelings for each other very often. Actually, when I think about it, not a day goes by that we don't say "I love you" to each other. And, trust me; it has not lost its effect even after ten years that we have been together. It sounds like a cliché but I don't really care. It is a cliché that I enjoy and I wish it upon everyone.

But, like I said, lately, she has been asking too often. Maybe she feels insecure for what lies ahead and she wants to confirm that I will be there, by her side, all the time. Maybe she is feeling the opposite. She is scared but she knows that I do love her and I will be next to her through the whole process from the moment of conception until… forever!

– Do you love me Yiannis?

I adore you my heart! You are my whole life. From the moment you entered my life ten years ago you have given a new dimension to things, I cannot exactly explain it. You have brought balance in my life. I can talk to you about anything and I feel that you understand me one hundred percent. I am never bored with you because you are both a pussycat and a tiger. The frills you do sometimes make me feel like the most brutal male on this planet. On the other hand, the dynamic character that you display at your work and in other aspects of your life make me proud to be by your side. I feel that together we can accomplish anything we aim for. I see you grow next to me and I do the same thing next to you and that makes life more interesting. I would stop a bullet with my body in order not to hit you my love!

August 18th, 2010   Week 14

Today I saw my parents off; they have been in Samos since August 2nd for a short vacation. They seem to have had a good time. My parents always have a good time on their holiday, wherever they go, whatever they do. I probably got it from them.

I had been looking forward to their arrival. I wanted to see them. I wanted to see their reactions when we would talk about the baby and see if they are anxious about their third grandchild and their first one from me.

The conversations between the two sets of in-laws and future grandparents were, as expected, very cliché and amusing. Stories from our childhood were proudly told with a sense of nostalgia. A specific expression, "I remember when…", was dominant in all the conversations as were also plans for the future and predictions about the baby. The baby's facial features will be like this…, if it is anything like Yiannis, it will not eat much and will be a skinny baby…, if it takes after my daughter, it will have beautiful almond-shaped eyes…and stuff like that.

Many parents-to-be are annoyed by such comments and all this obsession about the new member of the family. I agree that sometimes they can get exhausting and terrifying. They do, however, come from people who are more at ease with these things because they have already been through it and know what to expect. So, new parents out there don't get angry with your folks and pretend to be above all these "small-town", cliché behaviors. Because when the time comes to call your mother in a state of urgent panic to come over and help you clean the baby or show you how to calm it down after crying its little eyes out for no apparent reason, then you will be most grateful and you won't mind if they have one or more things to say about the baby.

I am glad my parents came to the island and lived this craziness with us, even for a little while. I wish to write some things about my parents but it isn't easy as I have so much to say and I am not sure how to structure it. I think the best way is to make a list of all the traits that I would like my kid to inherit from them.

Ladies first!

I would like it to inherit her self-confidence and self-assurance. This assurance stems only from the things she knows well and those she has already experienced. I would like it to be as cool and calm as she is during difficult times. Obviously, I would like it to inherit her spontaneity and great sense of humor. If it does, it will say funny and sometimes dirty jokes, it will carry out tasteful pranks and it will want everyone around it to laugh and be happy. If my kid takes after my mother, it will have strong doses of cold, calculating logic which will intertwine with and contradict her intense emotional rollercoaster rides and that will make for a very unpredictable and interesting person. One thing is for certain, that if my kid takes after its grandma, it will be a great friend and human being, one that you can count on for anything any time.

From my father, I would like it to inherit his optimism and the magical way he has of solving the problems that his family members face from time to time. If it takes after its grandpa, it will be very dynamic but in a discreet and low-key way and it will be very dear to everyone. It will be accepting and will have the best intentions for the people that it will deal with. But that doesn't mean that it will allow itself to be taken advantage of and that it won't know when to push some people out of its life. Of course, it will be very stubborn at times and very set in its ways but an apology and an act of good faith will open up the doors back into its life. It will run its family in a very efficient and democratic way and it will welcome everyone in its house. It will show its teeth, though, if it even has the slightest hint of suspicion that someone is trying to hurt any of its family members. And the best of all, it will know how to love its other half with incomparable respect and endless love, for when my father looks at my mother, the foundation of the greatest loves of international bibliography shake and all the women who have been loved greatly wonder: "Will anyone be able to love and adore me so much, so exaggerated, so unconditionally?"

August 19ᵗʰ, 2010

An incident today at the office made me remember the reason why I am noting down my thoughts in this diary.

A colleague referred to Father's Day, which is in June but I don't know how the conversation went there, in a very condescending and demeaning way. She was talking to one of my colleagues in my department and I happened to overhear their conversation.

I can't really blame her. She was very unlucky in picking the man who was going to be her husband and life companion, if you can call "companion" a man who beats his wife and children, who is a useless drunk and who functions and lives in our society as a parasite. It was more than once that she ended up in the hospital, abused and bruised. It was more than once that he came home drunk and took out his rage on his family, his wife and his four children. Why she had four kids with him is beyond me!

- Father's Day they say! Why should they celebrate and be celebrated? What did they do? We are the ones carrying the baby for nine months and we are the ones who care for it after and forever.
- You do have a point after everything you have been through but you should know that we are not all the same. For example, why shouldn't my father celebrate or my father-in-law or my brother? They are all excellent fathers and family men. Take Kostas (one of our colleagues) for example. His

wife dumped him and he is raising their son on his own with the help of his in-laws! Why shouldn't there be a special day for such people?

I felt bad having to point out to her so many examples of men that compare completely opposite to her ex-thank god-husband. But I just had to speak out and put things in the right perspective. I had to stand up for that portion of men who have been rocks for their families and who are examples to follow for the rest of us. At the same time I showed her that there is hope for her to find someone in the future, someone who will love her and her children and will treat them with kindness and dignity.

August 21ˢᵗ, 2010

During our first session with our doctor, he had told us that we can freely practice the most pleasurable of the marital duties, until a certain point in the term, of course, and we would have to take it easy. Practically, though, this presented challenges, at least for us.

The little foetus factory that is working overtime in my wife's belly has caused her an upset stomach. Besides feeling like vomiting, she feels her body changing. Even from a psychological point of view, when you know that a person is gradually being created inside you, how can you feel like it? As far as I am concerned, I have elevated my wife's body to divine status and I consider her to be a priestess of fertility. The classic, stereotypical thinking of "how can I dare defile all the above and do these things in the presence of my child" goes through my head very often. Yes, I admit it. I know that it is off base and although I am a modern, educated person who has seen the world, I can't stop thinking this way most of the time. Especially, when there is no green light from the other side.

Today, however, the green light came on and for the first time since we have found out we…the rest is unsuitable for minors and too personal for adults. The only thing I can say is that everything happened with a lot of caution, softly, gently and…beautifully!

August 22nd, 2010

Our first communication with the baby took place today. Rena had lied down on her side with her hand underneath her belly. That is when she felt a tap from inside.

– Hey, Yiannis, I just felt the baby.
– What? What happened? Let me feel, too!

She turned on her back and took my hand. She put it on the spot from which our little one came in contact with the outside world. I waited a while and then I felt a little tap, so light and faint. It was like a kid picking at you with its tiny finger; actually, that's exactly what it was! The feeling and the sensation was out of this world!

– What do you think our baby wanted?
– I don't know, maybe it's hungry and it is calling out to us: "hey you out there, is there anything to eat?"
– No, I don't think so. It probably just woke up and thought that it would play a little.
– Maybe even it wasn't comfortable and it changed position.
– Or because we have been talking but not about it, it wanted to draw back our attention.

— You think? It's gonna start that so early?

The speculations went on and they were very imaginative and funny.

Message received little one! We are looking forward to seeing you up close!

September 2010

September 1st, 2010   Week 16

"When I finally saw my daughter play piano at the school's concert, I couldn't but cry." Alexander said to me today when we met for a drink.

I am in Athens on a business trip so it was a good opportunity to meet with my good friend. Besides the teasing that I underwent from him regarding the fact that I will be a father and that the responsibilities, especially the financial ones, will never end, we also had a very serious talk about his relationship with his daughter. He described to me how much his behavior and attitude towards his daughter have changed ever since the child of a good friend of his, about 3 years old, has been hospitalized with a very serious illness.

– I have changed the way I see things since I heard. The only thing I care about any more is my daughter's well being and happiness. I used to put so much pressure on her to excel in school and to be perfect in anything she does. But she is only a child; I had no right to exert all this pressure on her. Sure I did it because I care about her and I wanted her to develop her potential as much as possible, but she can do that without the pressure. I never ask her what grade she got in an exam any more but whether or not she enjoyed what she studied and what she took out of it. I mean, I don't just ask her what happened at school or at music school or at her English class but I try to understand how she feels and how she perceives the things that take place in her environment. When she came home one day and told me that she no longer wanted to participate at the school's concert, inside me, I was furious. She is very talented and she had rehearsed for many hours for this concert. On the other hand, I could tell that she had been under a lot of pressure and she was exhausted by her busy schedule. So, I let her make her own decision of whether she will play at the concert or not. I didn't try to talk her out of it. Because of that, she felt I trust her decisions and she knew that I would be by her side no matter what she decided. A few days later and clearly more relaxed she announced her change of mind to finally take part in the concert. Not only that, she always made sure that she is never late for the rehearsals. When I finally saw my daughter play piano at the school's concert, I couldn't but cry.

I felt very proud of my friend today. As I sat there

listening to him fold out his emotions and narrating this story that made him change and be a better father, I thought that indeed two men can talk about more than just football or their work achievements or the global financial crisis. Two men can talk and share their concerns about fatherhood and learn from each other. I always knew that Alexander adored his daughter but today I saw something different in him. I realized how important his child's true happiness is to him and how much time he has devoted into having an inner dialogue in order to be able to change for her.

I felt great humility upon the grandeur of emotions that Alexander revealed to me and I now have a much higher appreciation of him. I am also relieved that now I know that I have someone to talk to, father to father, when I get "father's block" as my kid will be growing up.

September 9th, 2010

It was Laskarina's turn to meet with today. We met at the Metro station of Panormou and we walked for 2 minutes and reached this really great little square with cafés all around and we sat there to have a drink. I had never been there before. It was packed with young people, definitely younger than me, and the atmosphere was warm, cozy and sort of exclusive.

In the beginning we discussed about the current issues that we were facing at work, we always do that. I tell her about my successes and my fights at work and the news in the wine business and she lets me know of her own battles and successes in the difficult field of journalism and more specifically in chief editing.

I don't want to talk about their problem every time we meet but it would be hypocritical on my part not to, to pretend that it doesn't concern me. After all, I don't see her that often.

They are saving up for the artificial insemination that she had told us back in August and we shall see…

– Has this situation affected your relationship?
– Look, it isn't the easiest thing to deal with. It hasn't exactly had a bad effect on us but it has given a whole new meaning to love making. It is hard for me to make love without constantly having conception in my mind.
– That's understandable and until you have a child or until you reach a decision, whichever one that is going to be, that is how you will feel, unfortunately…how is Marios' behavior towards you?
– Great, as always, I really can't complain. To tell you the truth, Marios is not so set on having a child as I am. He says to me that his main concern is for us to be together…even if we never have a child…as long as we stay together.
– That's great! He loves you deeply, doesn't he?
– He does!...Still, I want a kid so bad Yiannis, I know I have so much love and so many things to give to a child. I want to pass down all these things that I have been through and all that life has taught me so far, to show it how to be a proper human being.
– You are going to be a great mother, I know it, and wait and see, the procedure in January will go very well and one year from now we will be talking differently, different issues. Can you imagine us, the four of us, taking out the strollers in downtown Athens for shopping,

both couples pushing the strollers with our bundles of joy inside? That would be a spectacle, wouldn't it?

— That would be so funny…you know what? I have a very good feeling for our next try.

— Yes, it will go great! Don't tell her I told you, but Rena said to me that this time you will probably make it and not miscarry. She has a great perception of things and from what we discussed in August she feels you are more ready and more experienced now. She asked me not to say anything so that I wouldn't give you false hope but Rena is almost always right about these things.

— Great…let's see what happens!

I was really pleased by our chat for two reasons. First of all, once again we have proof that my dear friend has found the right person in her life. Marios loves her very much to stand by her like he does. Maybe he wants a kid running around the house just as bad as Laskarina does but he tells her that he could do without so as not to put more pressure on her. Anyhow, he is a great husband and that is admirable.

The second reason I enjoyed our chat was that Laskarina seemed surer and more calm this time and that should help.

She got me thinking, though, too. "I have so many things to give to a child" she said to me. There is a need in us to transfer our experiences to a child, to help it avoid mistakes or at least be there by its side when it makes them. Why do we have this need though? Why do we want to even bother? It must be an instinct, the same instinct that made me get up off a chair to prevent a strange child from falling into the water once. He didn't fall in the water but seeing the little guy approaching the water and his parents having no idea what he was up to, both Rena and I instinctively sprung out of our chairs and went towards him. We only stopped heading his way when we were sure that he was out of danger. A primitive instinct from within made us react protectively towards a child that was not ours, the instinct of the continuation of the human race, I guess.

I assume that it is the same instinct that drives us to transmit our knowledge and experiences to the little creatures that look at us with doubt and admiration and expect guidance from us. But the one question raises another one. Do we consider ourselves to have acquired such wisdom and such composure in order to be able to function as mentors and guides of an innocent little soul that came in this world? Can any one say about oneself that they can handle the high level responsibility of raising a human being properly? Tough questions with even tougher answers.

This is why I believe that one must think really hard about the sacred burden of bringing a child into this world and not do it if not for the right reasons. Age doesn't play such a big part here, although with age comes wisdom, but internal peace and some serious soul searching. It is extremely important to know yourself as deeply as possible before you set on the journey of creating another Self, another personality who will basically walk on your footsteps. Can you pass on the right principles to another entity? If you can, do it, if not, wait.

— And what happens if the child is conceived by accident (I hate the expression "the child was an accident", what an insensitive thing to say) and you are not ready yet? Do you keep it or do you abort it?

As a rule, I am not for abortion. One question I often ask myself but I have not been able to answer definitively yet is whether one should keep a child that is going to be born with a mental disability so serious that it won't be allowed to fit in our society as it is structured today or a child that is diagnosed to be born with a serious physical disability. I don't know, things are not so clear to me in such cases but one should do what one thinks right. Each of these cases is unique and should be dealt as such.

However, I am clearly against abortion when the reasons are social or financial. And the main reason for that is because I am an avid fan and a strong supporter of the use of condoms. Let's start from there.

There is absolutely no reason for children to be conceived by accident and end up in special disposal bins at the hospitals just because two lovers were so enormously irresponsible and didn't use a condom or didn't use it right. They don't have the right. Excuses like "The passion overwhelmed us and we were not thinking straight" or "The condom broke, what could I have done?" are cheap and not suited to be spelled out by intelligent people nowadays. "Restrain yourself!" is my response to the one comment and "Pull out!" is my response to the second one and "...wear a condom and when you are about to climax pull out so that if it does break you will be outside the danger zone...so simple...it is not science!"

If you can't control yourself or are not willing to pull out and the woman does get pregnant, then you have two alternatives.

The first one is to accept your responsibilities and bring the little person into this world whether it completes your long-term relationship or is the result of a one-night stand. The circumstances under which it was conceived don't change the fact that an angel is coming to beautify this sometimes ugly world. You are obliged to realize what a great miracle it is to give life, the greatest miracle of all. It will be difficult in the beginning but you can make it. Life and nature have a way of settling things when the will is there.

— But I don't feel ready.
— No one ever is, it will come to you.

— But I am still immature.
— Grow up then, fast!

— But I am still a minor.
— That's all right, you've got parents. They must help you or they should have taught you to use a condom.

— But it will ruin my plans for a career.
— Bullshit! If your career has solid foundations, it will not spoil anything. After all, no career can compare to the miracle you are going to experience.

— But I will have to raise it myself.
— Many have made it; you will make it, too. Find a support system of relatives and friends.

— But I don't have the maternal instinct.
— Then you should have protected yourself from getting pregnant.

— But I don't know how to be a father.

> – You'll learn. If you know how to love, you will
> learn, nature will take care of it.

Many excuses! I can respond to all of them. I see, however, that you insist as I haven't managed to convince you. Let me present you with the second alternative, then.

You decide to have an abortion. You book your appointment with the doctor and you go to the hospital. The woman is laid back and they spread her legs open. At this point, allow me to remind you that in her womb a small person has started to take shape which, unsuspecting, is receiving nutrients from the umbilical cord and is growing. It feels warm and safe. It feels grateful to have such a cozy and hospitable environment to develop in and to prepare itself for coming out in a few months. Suddenly, you betray it. A hostile and unknown instrument enters its environment and starts searching. It is searching for it. It finds it and starts pulling violently. It cuts off any contact with the feeding system and takes it out of the place where a few minutes ago felt nice and warm. Its watery home is not hospitable any more. The baby feels undesirable and defenseless, it accepts its fate that in a couple of minutes it will simply be a lifeless mass which will be wrapped up and thrown in the hospital's trash.

Choose!

September 6*th*, 2010

Due to our baby not wanting to reveal its sex while we were in Athens, we thought to have another ultrasound exam, in Samos this time, one that was not scheduled. The doctor had a very hard time because our baby has a lot of energy and moves around in the belly a lot. 45 minutes later and sweating, he said to us:

« 90% chances it's a girl….!»

A girl! A beautiful baby lady which will have me run around for the rest of my life! It is foreseen that a great love will grow between father and daughter in this home. Is she going to do whatever she wants with me, I wonder? Will she be looking at me with her little eyes and act all cute and pretty with her little bow ties in her hair and I will succumb to her every wish? Is she going to be as beautiful and fashionable as her mother and will I be boasting as we are walking side by side on the street? The boys will stare at my gorgeous daughter and I will find reasons to reject them as the one will be a loser, the other one will be too needy, the other one will have an ugly beard and "who are these bums drooling over my daughter?". When she grows up, we will go for dinner, her mother, her and I and everyone will stare and the men will be envious as I will be the luckiest man alive escorting the most beautiful wife and daughter ever. I will take my daughter along in some of my business trips to show her the world and to teach her how to deal with the sexist pigs that are out there in the business world.   I will see her fall in love one day with the man of her dreams, the man she will replace me with. Will I be the standard of the man she is going to marry? Hopefully, or even better, someone much better than me, if that's possible!

Rena was hoping for a girl. She always told me that she wanted her first child to be a girl. She wants to pass on to her all those things that make a woman be a woman. She will definitely teach her how to respect herself and the people around her. She will want to teach her that an education and a sharp mind are important tools for a woman of today. She will show her how to match her clothes with her purse and her shoes and how to look dignified and charming. She will talk to her about how to take care of her husband but at the same time what to expect from him and that he should take care of her, too, if not more than she will. She will explain to her how important it is to be independent and to be able to stand on her own two feet at any given time. She will caution her to find a good guy to marry, someone who will treat her with love and gentleness, otherwise her crazy overprotective father will go take her back after he has beat the crap out of the loser who dared treat his princess badly.

A few days ago Rena confided in me that she had dreamt of our child. It was a girl with big eyes and long eyelashes. One part came true, we will have to wait and see about the rest.

September 18th, 2010   Week 18

This Saturday is very special to Rena and me. It was our first shopping spree for our baby.

The store is 30 minutes away from Karlovassi, where we live. It is in Vathi, where we both work. We preferred to go on a Saturday instead of staying after work during the week. This way we would have more time, we would be more relaxed and we would attach a more official air and significance to the first shopping spree for our daughter.

You get lost in there. There are so many things that a baby needs or make us think that it needs. You can stay in the store for endless hours looking at pacifiers, cots, sterilizers, cremes, powders, all kinds of highchairs and car seats, sheets, blankets, toys, clothes and many many other cute stuff, useful or not so much. Luckily, the lady that helped us was really good at her job and very patient with all our questions.

We ordered the pram-pushchair system which could very easily be one of the transformers since it changes and adjusts to so may different shapes for so many different uses.

You hold it like this, you push it like that, it can change into a carrycot, one thing clicks in, another clicks out. I am going to need seminars to be able to master it. We also ordered the cradle in which the baby will sleep in the beginning. The cradle is basically a small cot in which the baby rests for the first months for as long as the baby sleeps in the parents' room. We will order the regular cot later. The car seat comes with the pram, and its own price, of course, but in matching colors and fabrics and it clicks on the pram for more convenient transport of the baby. The bill along with some other stuff here and there came to 1.200 euros, close to 1.500 dollars, not at all a negligible amount!

This is why I advise the fellow fathers to maintain excellent relations with their parents and in-laws because this is the only way that the grandmas and grandpas will have the pleasure of offering their grandkid its first furniture or other useful things. If, for example, they offer to pay for the pram (600 euros!), as my parents did, who am I to deprive them of this pleasure?

September 22ⁿᵈ, 2010

Recently, I have been facing an issue with the export of our wines in Sweden and I have been in constant communication with one of the employees of our importer in an effort to resolve it. In the midst of all the e-mail exchanges he had to tell me that he wouldn't go to the office for a few days as his daughters are sick and he must stay home to take care of them. Probably his wife couldn't take the time off or he is a single parent, I didn't ask. I wrote to him about our pregnancy and that we are expecting a daughter and this is what he replied:

« Dear Yiannis,

Congratulations on your first child, I hope you and

your wife have a good and pleasant pregnancy. I will do my best to guide you if you need my advice, but having two daughters I now know that each child is unique. You think you know everything you need to know after the first one, but when the second one comes, you realize that you know only half of what you thought you did. The one thing that is certain is that nothing you have ever lived before will give you such happiness as the first time you see your child."

Who said that only Mediterranean people have strong, intense feelings about their families? It is said that people who live in warmer climates are more passionate and have warmer and closer relationships with their family members as they feel everything more intensely. However, in this case, our Swedish friend managed, in a single paragraph in a single e-mail, to give me advice that will be with me for the rest of my life as a father and will prepare me for the most important moments of my life.

And since our Swedish father referred to that special moment, I will never take out of my mind the image of my brother staring at his newborn daughter at the maternity clinic. When I entered the room of the clinic, I found Adonis sitting on the bed and having pulled close to him the plastic container his daughter was in. With his arms on the container and his head resting on them, he stared at his little girl with awe and curiosity. He didn't speak, to any of us. I greeted him but he didn't reply. He didn't seem to be n touch with his surroundings. His eyes were nailed on the baby and he was…just looking at it! It had seemed so strange to me that I remember the scene as if it was yesterday.

September 24th, 2010

I have been stressing out lately. I am worried that if

Rena goes into labor prematurely, I won't make it to the hospital in time and I won't be there.

Around December 15th, when Rena will be in month 8, her mother and she will move to Athens and will stay at their house in Moschato. Since we will have the baby in a private maternity ward in Athens, the doctor told us that she shouldn't travel through the 8th and 9th month. Therefore, she will have to leave Samos early. It is convenient for us since they have the apartment in Moschato, the apartment that will accommodate my pregnant wife and my impatient-to-be-a-grandma mother-in-law.

I will stay behind in Samos, for my work, of course. I will take a leave from work two weeks before the expected labor but what if it is premature? What if the water breaks earlier than expected and I don't make the flight to Athens in time? I don't want to miss these moments and I know that Rena wants me by her side. I can't even imagine my Rena going into labor and my showing up after the fact. I want to experience the waiting. I want to be there to try to convince Rena to let me be inside the labor room with her. I want to hear the nurse calling out my name to announce the good news. But since we chose to give birth in Athens, I will have to take my chances. I apologize to my wife and child in advance if I don't manage to be there. The guilt trips have already started.

I talked to Alexandros today and told him about my worries mentioned above. I asked him to take over in case I don't make it to fly to Athens. Obviously, the people who will stand in for me will be my father and my brother first. In case, however, they are not able to, Alexandros will go straight to the hospital to help out. My parents don't live in Athens any more, either. After their retirement, they moved permanently to our cottage in Korinthos which is an hour away from Athens. My brother is a night shift closings supervisor in a grand central hotel in Athens. Thinking and worrying about this, the first person that came to my mind after me and my family was Alexandros. I trust him completely and I am really glad he accepted the task. I hope I can repay him one day. He will probably never have to take over for me but just the fact that he accepted makes me indebted to him for a very long time.

September 30th, 2010   Week 20

I have been brought up with the notion that the relationship between a mother and a child can not be compared to any other relationship and that fathers can not have the connection that the mother has with the child. I didn't use to agree with the people that said that. On the one hand, I realized that a very strong relationship develops between them while the baby is in the womb, a relationship that a father can not conceive, naturally. On the other hand, I believed that from then on, after the birth, an equally strong relationship can develop with the father, too. I was wrong! Now I get it, now that I am living it, I understand now that I had no idea what I was talking about.

Our baby has started to move around in there and she has already established her ground rules. When Rena lies on her side, the little one doesn't like it and she taps her. Apparently, there are some positions in the belly with which she feels most comfortable. So, when Rena decides to switch sides and the baby doesn't like it, she taps her mother. Rena switches back to the original position, the baby calms down. The other day, Rena turned to me while we were in bed to tell me something and she was immediately informed by the baby that this was not an option.

— All right, little one, I will turn over, don't be like that!

That was the first time that Rena had talked to our baby girl so spontaneously and as if she was there. That exact moment was when I realized that they have already started developing a rapport, already through the belly. Rena has already started to compromise, to adjust her life, her movements, her thoughts according to the baby's needs. She is communicating with our tiny seed and together they negotiate their co-existence.

Yesterday, after we had turned off the lights, we were just about to fall asleep. We were both in that stage of the sleep where you are just starting to feel the heavy eyelids and the sweet numbness but you are not quite sleeping yet. In the darkness and the total quiet I suddenly heard Rena giggle. She stopped and then giggled again, a bit more loudly. I wasn't sure if she was awake or if she was having a dream.

— Rena?
— Yes?
— Are you sleeping, darling?
— No.
— What's with the laughing? Did you remember something funny?
— No, I didn't. The baby…!
— What about the baby?
— She is tickling me…from inside!

I also started laughing because the whole thing was cute and funny. At the same time, however, I felt outside of this special connection. What do I mean? The feelings and the contact that are being created between my Rena and the baby are so unique and so theirs that I can't understand them and Rena can't exactly share them with me. Not because she doesn't want to, it is just not possible. It is as if the two of them have created a private club in which no one else can enter. It's like when Rena and I are among strangers when we are out and we see or feel something funny or weird about someone we communicate with the eyes only and we understand each other without talking. This is very similar. Rena and the baby have agreed to a secret and special communication code.

Now, what should I do as a parent of secondary importance? Should I get angry? Should I be envious? Should I feel left out and start having feelings of escape from my home? This happens to many guys and they start looking for comfort and support in some other woman while their wife is pregnant. They feel that they are not their wife's primary concern or focus. But that's how it is, that's how it should be! Accept it already and deal with it! This is not so bad, fellow dads-to-be. It's completely normal, that's what I think.

So, instead, of running away from your home and looking for confirmation and a "lick" in the wounds of your inflated and hurt ego, claim today a small part in this magical relationship. Talk to your wife and tell her how you feel. Following is a theoretical dialogue:

- Honey, I feel a bit left out.
- What do you mean?
- You know, with the baby. You talk to it and you can feel it inside you and I am just a viewer who doesn't get what is going on.
- I see where you are coming from, but don't feel left out. What's happening between me and the baby is something special and different.

- I know. I am jealous.
- Come on baby, don't be. Aren't you the one who got me pregnant and now we are living this miracle together…sure, it's more of a miracle for me, but we can't fight nature.
- Could you let me know when the baby is moving or poking you so that I can put my hand on you and feel the baby, too?
- Of course!

Sometimes things are so simple and we choose to make them more difficult. The expression "Sit back and enjoy" is perfect for this situation. Dads-to-be should relax and enjoy what is happening before their eyes. If it's too early to claim a more important part in our relationship with our baby as fathers, let's be supportive observers of the wonderful interaction between the little one and the woman who is carrying it and we will have infinite opportunities to establish ourselves in its little heart once it is born. After all, we are men, not nagging, crying babies!

October 2010

October 3rd, 2010

$\mathscr{I}$ am writing in the plane on my way to Kiev, Ukraine. I am urgently leaving to represent the wines of Samos in an exhibition that is taking place there these days. It wasn't a scheduled trip for me but due to a last minute issue that came up and my superior had to stay back to deal with it, I was asked to replace him. My position at the winery, Sales Manager, requires me to travel a lot and attend some wine fairs in Greece and abroad.

This is my first trip abroad ever since we found out that Rena is pregnant. I had already prepared her that I might be asked to go to this trip last minute. The reason I did that is because she doesn't like it when I am away, now in her condition. She feels insecure and she wants me constantly on her side. I also felt very weird today at noon when I left the house for the airport. Knowing that Rena and her little stuffing will stay back, as I was driving away I had the impression that there was a rubber band that was wrapped around my waist and was pulling me to go back. There is no other way, though, my job requires me to travel often and we must get used to this…all three of us now.

We took off a little while ago. I always say a short prayer when we take off and touch the cross that I always wear. "God, let me arrive well to my destination and let me return safely to my wife", I used to say. This time, unconsciously, I added the phrase "…and child" in the end. Yeah, it sounds nice! Let me return safe to my wife and child. My eyes got all watery thinking that every time I will leave from now on I will be flooded by a feeling of nostalgia and sweet joy for the return.

When I travel, I always make sure to bring back a gift for Rena, it is sometimes a cheap traditional souvenir, she likes key chains and those glass balls that are filled with liquid and "snow" or silver dust and depict the most famous landmarks of a place. Most of the times, though, it is designer clothes or purses and usually brands that you can not find in Greece or I find cheaper abroad. She has many things from me that have come from different corners of the world to the great satisfaction of the credit card companies with which I have had a perfect cooperation all these years!

From now on I will have two women in mind when I go shopping, Rena and my baby girl. In this way I will compensate my daughter for my absence. If she gets upset when I leave, at least she will know that daddy is going to come back with a present. When she grows up though some of those presents she will buy herself because I intend to take my kids with me on my work-related trips, not all of them of course, maybe once a year.

I look forward to the time when I take my kid with me on a business trip in any one of the grand capitals of the world. I will show her all the airport procedures and explain to her their purpose and I will guide her how to choose the right hotel. She will join me at the exhibitions to see what it is like to talk to people for 8 hours straight and what it's like to make efforts to promote and sell your product. In the evenings, we will visit the city sights and go shopping for things that are different and representative of where we will be. I will show her how to choose nice restaurants for dinner and I want to initiate her in international cuisine and show her how to have good, original food without paying a small fortune. I will talk to her about how to keep herself safe and how to walk around in a strange city and how to avoid being a victim of…I can't even think about it or write it down…but I have to talk to her about it. I will point out to her the arrogant business men-pigs that in the future will try to treat her more as a woman than a professional woman. Yes, my daughter will face such issues. She is going to be so gorgeous that she will have to keep proving to others that she also has the brains to do her job very well. How do I know that she is going to be both gorgeous and smart? That's easy; all you have to do is look at her mother!

Travelling is nice but if I had a different kind of a job, one whose prerequisite wasn't all the trips, I wouldn't have to leave every now and then and miss important moments from her growing-up. Should I look for another job?

How difficult is it for a man to start looking for a job during such a sensitive time in his family's life? I, for example, am quite satisfied with my job in terms of responsibility and significance in the company and I receive a satisfactory salary. Although no salary is ever correspondent to the tasks of a hard--working employee, the work schedule is very humane and rare in our days, 7-3. I may wake up really early but I am home early afternoon and I can spend time with my family for the rest of the day. This also gives me time to do other stuff, for myself, too,. not just for my home.

When you are expecting a child and you have a good job, then you are basically "stuck". Always theoretically speaking, if, for some reason, I thought about starting to look for something different, I don't know if I would go through with it. I wouldn't want to risk it since I already have a good thing going. My priority now is not so much my job satisfaction or the level of initiatives I can take or any of those job components that provide one with fulfillment. At the age of 36 and after 17 years of work experience, I am at my peak right now and I can be very creatively effective with my work. Whether I will be able to apply my ideas or not is not that important any more. What is crucial, is for me to provide financial security to my own people, my loved ones, the family unit that my wife and I are about to extend.

Fortunately, I don't need to look for something else. I love what I do! Wine has given me so much in so many different levels, tangible and intangible.

It saddens me to think of those people who are starting their family nowadays, in one of the greatest financial crises that Greece has ever been in, and they work for much less money than I do. They may be forced to get a second job. Their other half is working, too, but sometimes two paychecks are not enough. With money being scarce, grandparents are recruited to help out with the babysitting because hiring someone is not an option. I take my hat off to those people who have to get out there and work two jobs from morning to night in order to raise their children.

The downside, though, is that they don't get to see their children as much as they should or as much as they would want to and their absence could affect the development of the child's personality. That is when the father, the father usually gets the second job, must do everything possible to find some time to devote to his children. It is hard, but he must find the physical strength and mental capacity to spend some quality time with them. He must let them know that he would like to spend more time with them but it is not possible for the time being and explain to them that the few moments he sees them, plays with them and talks with them are the most important moments in his day. He must assure them that they play the most vital role in his life regardless of where he spends most of his time.

I am wondering, considering the rising unemployment and with the economic situation developing as it is, if it would be better for all of us to redefine our priorities. Maybe we can live with less consumer goods. Maybe it's better to live with less but actually live life. Wouldn't it be better for the second child to wear the first one's used clothes but have both its parents at home in the evening? Do you think that it is more precious for a child to own one of those damned computer games that suck its brain out than sit down with mom and dad and play a board game or go for a family walk at the park?

The only thing that our angels need in huge amounts is love. Love is free, you don't have to travel far to get it, it is endless, it does not require special storing or maintenance conditions and goes great with care and devotion, also free. Trust me, if there is love, everything else, I won't say that it will come easily or even come at all, but it will eventually be solved in one way or another.

October 5th, 2010

This morning, half an hour after I had woken up, I had my first serious guilt trip.

When I got up in my cold hotel in freezing Kiev, I immediately started getting ready for a busy day. I kept thinking that I needed to bathe, dress, have breakfast and before I left for the exhibition hall to check my e-mails and see what is going on back at the office. In all that, I suddenly remembered that I have a wife and an unborn child back in Greece. I was shocked at myself and my knees went numb. Why weren't Rena and our baby my first thought when I woke up? I was very upset with myself and I started calling me names and feeling disappointed in me.

– Nice going Yiannis, are you the same person who has been spending hours writing about your feelings about the baby's arrival and talk so warmly about family and love for children? You found yourself away from home for a while and your business concerns took first place in your head. Your first thought should have been how your wife slept the previous night, if she was kept up by the baby moving around inside her, if the baby is all right and if she is continuing to communicate in her own special way. Yes, surely you are obliged to focus on your work, especially being the first day of the exhibition, to make sure that everything runs smoothly and represent the winery as deserved, but this is for 3 days while your family is for ever.

Guilt filled my head and I began to realize that this business trip served as an outlet for me to get away from the constant worrying about the pregnancy and the coming of the newborn. It was a slap in my face, by my own hand. And that is when I thought that I was experiencing my first wave of guilt for not being there, not watching Rena grow bigger and telling me what news we have from the Belly.

I don't know, I won't be able to resolve this with myself

today. I want to work on it a while and let my brain process it a bit, see what went wrong. I was upset…very upset!

October 8ᵗʰ, 2010

Returning from Kiev today, I never expected the trip back to be so interesting. You can never guess how intriguing or indifferent your day is going to be.

One of the members of the delegation to Kiev was a business man from Samos who I got to know better there. On the way back, we had the opportunity to talk a lot. Things worked out in such a way that the only ones who returned to Samos the same day were the two of us.

He is around my age and his wife is due for their first child in November. They are having a boy…a future candidate husband for my daughter! We got to talking about fatherhood and it was as if I was looking at and talking to myself in the mirror.

He told me that he has never felt this way ever in his life and this phase of his life is more wonderful than he had imagined. The way he looks at his wife has changed; he loves her even more now and considers very sacred what is happening to them. He, too, felt that he changed as a person when he heard his baby's heart for the first time. I was stunned as I heard him talk to me and open up to me so easily. I kept nodding and saying "Me, too", "Same here!".

To confirm what he was telling me about all the love and respect he has for his wife was the way that he talked to her when she called him. He was so gentle and sweet with her and he talked to her as if no one else was around. It was as if the world had stopped moving and he immersed into the conversation with her. She probably expressed some of her concerns and insecurities over the phone because he kept reassuring her, "…everything is going to be OK…", "…that's not even a problem, don't worry…".

They have also rearranged their life to accommodate the new little one. He has arranged to have the time off work when his wife has the baby. He wants to be at home, too, to help out and support his wife. They have hired a male midwife. "A what?", I asked. "A male midwife!", he answered and with the question mark still hovering over my head he went on to explain to me that there are male midwives and that is what they are actually called. I had had no idea that there were men that did that. He said that he is really good at what he does because he has experience of his own as he is married with children. He guides his pregnant wife step by step and he has become part of their family.

I was very moved to hear my new friend talk with such ease and with such flow about what he is experiencing and what a dedicated father he is planning on being. I was left speechless, though, when he told me that the day their child was conceived, he knew.

- You are joking!
- No, I am not!
- Me, too! I knew it, too, not the exact day but around those days that we actually conceived I was very certain that we had made it.
- I knew the exact day that it happened.
- Incredible!
- Yes, isn't it weird?
- Exceptionally weird, you are the first man that I have heard admit it besides my brother.
- Your brother, too?
- Yes! I didn't dare tell anyone besides my wife in fear of people thinking I've gone mad.

Can we summon a scientist to enlighten us on what is going on here? Is it possible that us men have such kind of sensitivity to know when our swimmers have reached the desired destination? Usually, women are the ones who have such instincts and premonitions.

An excellent day today! My delight for talking to this man today is huge. I felt part of a silent society of men who will be or want to be amazing fathers and very justified to be writing my thoughts down.

October 10ᵗʰ, 2010

It seems that most of the conversations we have with Rena about our child, we have them in bed. I noticed it while writing this diary.

Yesterday, in bed during the afternoon siesta, I was remembering the day in Kiev when, preoccupied with business, I felt guilty about not having my little girl and my wife on my mind all the time. Amazing how much this has affected me and how badly it has made me feel! It is just as well though that it happened this early so that I can realize my responsibilities and set my priorities.

- Rena, do you think I will be a good father?
- Yes, darling, I am sure.
- Really?
- Yes, but make sure that you will be able to say "no" to the little one now and then!
- Mmmm…

I do want my daughter to become assertive as long as she is not too much of a smooth operator with me. Everyone tells me that the role of father really suits me and that I will be good at it. I am not sure what it is about me exactly that make them say this to me and most of the times they say it without thinking about it too much. Maybe it is the element of protectiveness that I have for the people in my world, my family, my friends, even my colleagues at work.

It is many times that I have become a raging bull in order to defend a member of my family, especially my wife. I will never forget the physical strength that I found in me to push back onto a wall this tall man who was drunk and stoned and tried to strike Rena. I was quick enough to get in front of Rena and I threw him on the wall. And considering I am 1,70 meters tall and 70 kilos heavy, that is a feat.   But even for my colleagues, especially the ones who work in my department, I have never let anyone else from the other departments, or our manager, offend them professionally or deprive them of any of their rights.

Maybe it's the way that I communicate and click with kids when I am around them. I find talking to kids intriguing and I consider it a challenge to "unlock" the communication codes of each kid. I always try to teach them something and I always try to learn something from them. If one sits down and talks to a child and observe its physical behavior as well as its sayings, one will discover a whole school. Children haven't learnt to filter what they say. They shoot out little words expressing their thoughts spontaneously and one can discover that the truths that children talk about are the simplest and the most definite.

A strange phenomenon that I have noticed myself happening is the way I photograph when I take pictures with babies. Generally, I am not very photogenic, but in the pictures that I have taken with my godson and other babies or young children, I look really good. It is probably my aura that softens up when I am around children. The joy of being with them is internal, honest and innocent as innocent are the souls of little children.

We shall see…! I will definitely try to be a good father.

October 16ᵗʰ, 2010   *Week 22*

We are in Athens for yet another ultrasound exam. We get to see our baby in a few days, on the 20ᵗʰ, Wednesday, "LIVE…from the Belly…we present to you the Baby Girl… live today in our amniotic studio…you will see hands moving, legs kicking, mouth opening and closing and much more…on Wednesday the 20ᵗʰ here on Belly TV". My brain spins curiously sometimes.

Besides the ultrasound, we have a lot of other chores. We have to tidy up Rena's home in Athens to be ready to welcome Rena and the baby when it is born. My mother-in-law had arranged for the house to be painted before we get there so that we will find it fresh and bright. Naturally, the painters had to move all the objects of the house in the middle of the floors away from the walls.

So, today, when we arrived to the house from the port, what do we see? A freshly-painted house? Not only that! Mounts of clothes and carpets and all sorts of sheets and blankets stacked up on furniture which was pulled in the middle of the floors away from the walls. The same picture was in all the rooms, a complete chaos. Paintings and picture frames were all taken off the walls and left scattered everywhere and anywhere. It is a good thing that I didn't have to deal with all that straight away because it was Saturday and we had to hurry to go shopping for a bed. On Sundays, stores are closed, so we left the mess behind until the evening.

For Saturday night we arranged dinner in a nice little

taverna with Loukia, Stamatis and their newborn Panos and Maria, Rena's cousin. We kissed, we hugged and all of our attention was immediately turned to baby Panos. He has grown so much since the last time we saw him. Now he is 3 months old and he is at that stage of starting to become chubby and squeezable. The facial features are more distinct now and you can tell who he takes after. He looks a lot like Loukia but has the facial expressions of Stamatis. After we all held him and played with him a bit, he remained quiet in his stroller looking at all of us and eyeing us. His gaze is still not very steady but you can tell that he is trying to focus his little eyes on our facial features. When I held him, I goggled my eyes as I was talking to him. That's how I distracted him when he was restless or about to cry. He had started nagging because he was hungry and while Loukia and Stamatis were preparing his milk, the rest of us tried to get his mind off his hunger so that he wouldn't start crying his little lungs out in the crowded tavern.

The happy parents seemed better than they were during our last visit, more rested. The little man sleeps almost through the whole night so the sleep-deprived parents can now rest their tired bodies. Apart from the signs of rest on their faces, tight skin and rosy cheeks, I noticed something different about them that I am realizing right now that I am writing and bringing back in my mind the images of them. I saw all three of them being very close and tight. What I mean is now you could easily tell that they were a family. Apparently, they had gone over the stage where you bring the baby home and you wonder "Who is this little person that we brought home with us and is defining our lives? Before, it was just the two of us having a good time and now we have this little poop machine that keeps us awake at night and demands 100% of our attention". Last time we saw them, you could tell they were at that stage. Obviously, they loved their baby and would do anything to take good care of him but you could sense that they had been invaded in a sudden and almost violent way. But now, it was clear that the two plus one had become a wholesome three. Watch and learn Yiannis! You are just about to get there!

Stamatis, a conscious father now, was calm, serene, serious. He was proud of his child and the unity of his family. He smiled satisfied of what was going on around him and he kept peaking in the stroller where his son was laying. He asked me how I felt that the time is coming and I told him that other times I am very happy and others terrified not knowing what to expect. He reassured me that we will work it out as they did and we continued feasting.

There was something that Stamatis told Rena that I kept as very important. Rena was talking to Loukia asking her how things are three months later. Stamatis cut in and told her in the same serene and settled down air that I mentioned before: "Your life will change, Rena. This is something… very different". He turned and looked at his son who was in Loukia's arms and concluded, "He grows up and you grow with him, right Panos?"..

I think that with what he said he answered a question that I have always had, "Why do parents always say that after they had their first child a new life started for them? Why do they feel that their life before the child was just a preparation period for this new chapter?". Because they grow differently with a baby in the house. But I don't want to analyze this and imagine it any further, I'd rather wait and live it!

October 17ᵗʰ, 2010

Today was a day of house chores, many house chores. By nighttime we had managed to straighten up and make the house presentable. Only a few details were left to be taken care of by Rena and her mother who is arriving tomorrow for back up. Rena was the grand coordinator and I was the humble, happy-to-be executor because the chores were heavy and in no way could she do any of them in her condition.

We did have a nice break in the afternoon as we had arranged lunch with my parents and my brother's family in a restaurant known for its great meats. This restaurant is situated in this area called "Vlahika" where you find a series of restaurants, all next to each other, serving nothing but delicious and proficiently-cooked meats, mostly barbequed. It was my mother's idea to get all together and eat out. We hadn't visited this "historic" area, where the meat-eating orgy is legendary, for ages. I am not complaining, the roasted pork and the barbequed lamb with all the accompaniments were excellent!

Also excellent was the family setting. My parents sat together at the end of the table and besides their food they were also enjoying watching their children with their families talking and exchanging news. Rena was talking to my brother's wife and I sat among my brother and nieces and we were talking. Sia, my eldest niece, who is in the third class of Junior High, was telling me with great determination what she has decided to do when she finishes High School. She aims to be a physicist or a chemist, not to teach but to work in a lab. She is thinking about studying abroad as she is not very satisfied with the educational system in Greece. Vassilikoula, the youngest, who is in the first class of Elementary school, was telling me about her secret diary and a group of girls that she belongs in, called "Super Girls". The "Super Girls" have secret powers.

 – What kind of secret powers do you have?
 – We run fast, we are smart, what else…?

    — Can you fly?

    — No!…oh I remembered…another secret power
        we have is that we never fight!

I couldn't believe what I was hearing. The secret power of those six-year-olds is that they never fight and they always get along. Do I really need to write any more about how much we can learn from children? There you have it, such deep knowledge from a cute little girl whose backpack contains a secret diary, crayons and markers and several other things that remain secret and she never parts with.

Adonis and Sia kept teasing each other. It is an ongoing game they have between them which made me hold my stomach from laughing and left me impressed as to how much Sia takes after my brother. They are both quick-witted and they never let anything go by without a smart or smart-ass comment.

The little one kept stealing the spotlight with her grace and her pirouettes that she has been taught at ballet. Her big sister was looking at her without even a trace of jealousy; I would even say that she was almost maternal to her. After all, she helped out a lot in her raising.

My heart was content! I felt grateful to my parents for their organising this family outing. I was especially glad that while my nieces don't see Rena and me too often, they were eager to talk to us and get to know us better. They didn't feel awkward around us, which means that we are included in their daily conversations and they know well that they have an aunt and uncle in Samos, an aunt and uncle that are preparing a little cousin for them.

October 18ᵗʰ, 2010

" My dear baby girl,

This letter is the first one that I am writing to you and I felt the need to write it to give you an overview of what is going on in the house in Moschato right this minute. If you were out of the Belly and sitting here with me, we'd have good laughs together.

So, check it out! I am sitting at the desk at the end of the living-room in front of the laptop writing you these lines. Your mama and grandma are taking care of the household and you should know that it's all being done in your honor, as we are expecting you. And all this for your stay which is going to be only a month after you are out and two months before you come out. We have already painted the house, we have got rid of much useless stuff and my back is aching because of all the clothes and things that I had to carry from one closet to the other. Anyway, the heavy chores are finished.

The most entertaining part is to watch your mother and your grandmother Thome trying to decide how to decorate and where to place all the little things in the house. Your grandma is suggesting and your mother is rejecting. Your grandma, although she doesn't agree with your mother, can't argue too much with her because she has got you inside her and we are not supposed to upset her. Grandma is decorating the kitchen counter, the tables and the shelves with all sorts of objects, useful and not, and your mother is always one step behind her taking everything down and saying that this style is too heavy, too busy and out of style and "…it's gonna be like an antique store in here…" Grandma wants to hang up double drapes and your mother, who is a fan of minimal decoration, nags and insists that the house should have a lighter feel. Obviously, your mother gets her way.

To be honest, your mother has a great sense of style and the house has become very cozy and charming. She has set everything up in such a way that she feels comfortable for as long as she is going to be here and for you to see when you arrive. There…your mother just threw out a vase behind your grandma's back. Then she turned and winked at me cause she knows I am watching them. I love your mother very much…just letting you know!

Today your grandma bought you your basket, your first little bed. With that we will bring you home from the hospital. Besides the basket, she got you two bibs and a little basket for your toiletries. Everything is matching, of course! So far, you have your super pram-pushchair from grandma Vasso and grandpa Adonis and your Moses-basket from grandma Thome and grandpa Paris who will probably buy you the cot-bed too. I am just letting you know so that you can thank them when you pop out of the Belly. .

Oh oh, now your mom is arguing with your grandma because grandma wants to put all these little decorations on the counter and your mom just wants to put a platter. Your mom wins again and peace is back

I wish to ask you a favor. If possible, don't kick your mom too much during the night because she can't sleep. Kick as much as you want during the day. If it's not possible, see what you can do. Also, I want to ask you to do what you do when you tickle your mother and she starts laughing out of the blue. She gets so sweet when that happens and so beautiful when she laughs like that, like a little girl.

Closing this letter, I want you to know that we are very happy to see you at the sonogram in a couple of days. We already love you very much and we can't wait to hold you in our arms in a few months. Take care in there and communicate often!

With a lot of love,
Dad

P.S.: I will ask your mother to also write you a letter so you can have a letter from both of us while you are still in the Belly."

October 20ᵗʰ, 2010

The word "moment" is defined in the dictionary as "a brief time". But how we define a moment of joy or a moment of agony or a moment of terror depends on how each of us perceive facts that concern us and touch us. A moment could be a minute or a second. A moment of joy can last very little while it is happening but you will remember it for ever. The effect of it on your body and soul will remain indelibly printed in your brain. A moment of fear, when you feel the world around you crumble like a tower of cards, can last for a very long time as you live every single second of it and you wish for time to turn back. You wish for this to never have happened. You do not want it to become part of your memory cells but it will. All you can do is put it in its little box in your head and move on…and thank God it is over!

I am worn out, myself and my wife and our baby. My body is beat; my eyes are constantly wet, ready to burst in crying. My heart is filled with joy and fear simultaneously. My soul was fed with moments today, moments of excitement but moments of agony, too. The latter ones didn't pass quickly, damn it! Every second seemed like a minute, every minute like an hour. I am worn out…but I will write to exorcise the bad moments and to make them go away.

A team of experts tried to explain to us today, more to me than Rena because of her profession, what Ventricular Septal Defect (VSD) in the heart of our baby means. It was the doctor who did the sonogram and discovered it, the special child cardiologist who accepted to see us last minute and do a more thorough examination, Rena's gynaecologist, who all tried to inform us of what it means for our baby to have a tiny "hole" in its heart.

Our appointment for the exam was at 11:30 this morning. Again, we were there half an hour earlier for the date we had with our little girl. We had to confirm that it was a girl because during the last sonogram in Athens last time, we couldn't tell what it was. A doctor related to Rena did a sonogram in Samos and gave us chances of 90% that it is a girl. The doctor in Samos had been right! Half a minute after the exam started, our baby did a flip in the Belly, very skillfully I dare add, and she showed us her all. I immediately recognized it. I pointed first to the screen and I said, "Oops, there it is, it's a girl!". The doctor agreed and she zoomed in on that key part of women, for which wars have started. In the beginning, I felt a bit awkward looking at my daughter's "pipi" but after I got over it I felt so proud of her and then I felt rage for all those inexperienced, pimple-covered teenagers who, when the time comes, all they will have on their brain will be her "pipi". Yes, they will, but they don't know who her father is and how I will have schooled her to deal with them and how I will devour them if they try to hurt my little girl. I am off the subject now.

The doctor went on with the examination with her assistant next to her recording the figures that she was telling her and we were happy to have confirmed the sex of the baby and that everything seemed fine. We saw her hands and counted her little fingers, five in each hand. We saw her little foot and made jokes because the feet in my wife's family are sort of enlarged. We saw her holding her feet with both hands and we were lucky enough to see her face on a three-dimensional coloured picture on the screen. Although her face was stuck on the placenta and her facial features weren't that discernible, she was so beautiful and she had such big lips!

Happy moments, short and unforgettable!

I began to worry when I noticed that the doctor had focused on the area of the heart and she persisted. Her faint smile that she had during the examination before had turned into a restrained concern. And she persisted… and she kept looking…at nothing else but the heart. Rena had also started frowning and knew that something was wrong. I wanted to ask the doctor if she had discovered something that requires concern but I was afraid of the answer that I would get. I didn't want an answer, none. The only words out of her mouth that I wanted to come out were "…everything is great guys, we will see you next time!". Instead of that I heard her tell Rena something about VSD in the heart of the baby and she had to send us to a special child cardiologist at a big clinic on Monday for a more detailed examination. Rena became anxious and tried to break down the communication codes of her colleague in order to figure out if we really had something serious to worry about. The doctor reassured us that she doesn't think it is something serious and she is sending us for the more thorough examination preventively. But, today is Wednesday, who can wait till Monday. I have to leave for Samos tomorrow.

When Rena went into another room to change I asked the doctor to arrange the special sonogram by the special doctor for today. She called her and she told us to leave immediately and go to Kifisias street, where her office is. The cardiologist was about to leave her office but our doctor asked her to wait and she accepted. We took a taxi and we asked the driver to go to Kifisias as fast and safely as possible which was a difficult thing to ask since it was already noon and the traffic was heavy. In the taxi, the time wouldn't pass. I was still relatively cool thinking that we shouldn't worry yet because nothing was definite. Rena was deep in her thoughts and I imagine that she was trying to remember from her medical books and from her experience at the hospital the implications of this defect and what that would mean for the life of our child. In such cases, ignorance may be better for the ignorant one. For the other one, though, who is not ignorant and has the capacity to know the best and worst case scenarios, knowing can be a nightmare. And my Rena was living a nightmare during those endless moments in the taxi. I was feeling awful knowing that Rena was spinning all the possible scenarios in her head and she didn't share her thoughts with me. She wouldn't tell me what would be the worst to expect. I was just holding her hand and kept telling her, "You will see, it's nothing, and if it is something, we will deal with it together…". But I have no clue, how do I know that everything is going to be all right? I can only hope. Ignorance labours hope and suddenly you become religious again and you leave the matter into the All Mighty's hands.

At last, the taxi arrived. During the ride, Rena found the courage to explain some things to me and to inform me that even if we are dealing with a more serious problem, that is, if the little hole in the heart hasn't closed by the time she is born, there will be an operation later on in her life and it will close. She added that many babies are born with the so-called murmur and if it doesn't correct itself, the surgeon will.

We went up to the doctor's office and we thanked her for accepting to see us last minute. She was very cool and she seemed composed and that was sort of comforting, I felt more at ease. We entered the sonogram room and the routine procedure started again. In a little while we would find out what was going on and what we needed to do to take care of our child. No, not yet, the agony had to be prolonged. Our little one was positioned inconveniently and she would not move.

- Guys, I can't see the heart the way she is positioned, we have to make her turn around or you can come back Monday.
- Make her turn around, definitely, not Monday, we need to know now…please...if possible!.

She told us to go to he nearest coffee shop and have Rena drink the sweetest chocolate drink she could find, not go to the bathroom at all and walk up and down the street for about twenty minutes before we try again. The sugar from the chocolate drink would make the baby move and change positions, our baby was about to have her first sugar rush. So we did. Rena drank that sweet mix and we walked up and down Kifisias street. We passed outside a church and the only thing that I could pray for was for the waiting not to be extended and for the baby to turn around so we could see her little heart.

We returned to the office and, luckily, the examination could start, the baby was moving in there. Along with the examination started my own, personal nightmare. My eyes were lifted up on the screen which was above me and I was thinking that that was the moment we would find out what was wrong, or not. Many thoughts, bad thoughts, too bad to write down, were going through my head. These were thoughts that in no way did I want to connect to the health and condition of my child. I even started wondering what would happen if we were advised to terminate the pregnancy. My sweet God, what would we do? How would we cope with something so terrible? I almost heard my heart shatter in thousands of pieces. My blood froze and the moments of sheer horror would not pass. What I was feeling was no longer agony and concern, or even fear, it was utter and complete horror. I looked at the wet eyes of my Rena and I wanted us to pass to another dimension, not to be living what we were living. My Jesus, please let my child be ok and I can't ask for anything more! But, what went wrong? Everything was perfect up to now. The baby was developing beautifully, able-bodied and healthy. What went wrong or why should something have to go wrong?

The doctor was searching and searching and didn't speak. I don't think I have ever had to be so patient in my entire life. I was watching the doctor and it was as if I had my Creator across from me. Her expression was formal, frozen, professional. Surely, countless couples with the same fears as ours had passed by her office and she was perfectly trained not to show any emotion during the examination so that her expression changes wouldn't be misinterpreted. She knew very well that I was hanging from her every word and that to me she seemed like God in heaven. She knew very well that I was anxious to see an encouraging nod of the head or a reassuring smile on her lips.

–   Well guys, we have nothing to worry about. The VSD is so tiny that other equipment would not even be able to trace it. I think we have fallen victims of our state-of-the-art equipment. They show details that conventional sonograms wouldn't and that is the only reason you are here today.

Rena started talking to her in medical terms. The fact is that this happens to many babies and the reason why the first doctor was slightly worried was because by this week in the pregnancy the Ventricular Septal Defect should have closed or be much smaller. The doctor said that it is so tiny that she won't need to see us again; however, we did tell her that we will check again in December. In case it does not close, our little girl will have to undergo a routine operation at the age of seven, an operation that is considered routine and quite easy for surgeons nowadays. She reassured us that the baby will have a normal development even if she is born with this little abnormality in her heart.

The blood started flowing in my veins again. I was white from fear until we heard the good news. My Rena was relieved also. My poor Rena! How scared she must have been, too! I remember her when we met, me at the age of 26 and her at 21. Back then, she was a girl with no cares besides her studies and now she was the same beautiful face but with the burden of motherhood on her shoulders.

Our day wouldn't end here because we had an appointment with the gynecologist at 5, where we would have to relive the day's events and he would tell us not to be upset and all those nice words that would sound to us like little pleasant-sounding, joyfully-ringing bells.

It was 3 in the afternoon when we grabbed a taxi to go back to Moschato to eat and regroup before we go to the doctor's. My wide sunglasses were covering my eyes but couldn't hide the slow-flowing tear streams that were running left and right of them. These were tears of relief. This was a quick trip to hell and back, from noon till 3, thank God, it could have been worse!

I am exhausted…! I am going to crawl into bed with Rena. I will hug her and with my one hand on her belly I will sink into a lethargy of gratitude and relief.

October 21st, 2010

Each time I travel and reach my destination I call Rena

or text her. She wants to know the time that the plane landed and that I am well and, basically, she wants to know that the plane actually landed. She has a phobia when it comes to air travel. It is not her favorite thing to have to fly often and, naturally, she is also worried about me.

I had told her the day before that I would text her instead of calling her as I would land at 8 am and I didn't want to disturb her sleep. When I text her, she hears the beep, she reads the text and falls calm back to sleep.

This time my text was longer, it contained more words.

"I landed baby! All is well! Kisses to you and our baby girl!"

In the text I included for the first time our unborn child. It wasn't studied, I did it without thinking about it. It came to me very naturally at that moment to think about both my girls. I didn't consider this text and the inclusion of the baby as just another text and if you have come to know me at all from the previous pages, then you must expect me to analyze this. And that's exactly what I am going to do!

A little while ago, I was feeling a bit detached from the relationship that had started to form between Rena and our child. I felt like a spectator and not an active participant. I am assuming that, due to yesterday's events, I am beginning to connect with the baby. Yesterday, all three of us, as a family, got moving to find out what is wrong with one of us. We had to make the impossible possible in order to protect this little creature that we are about to bring into this world, without even asking it. Surely, I would have preferred to have bonded with the baby as a result of a moment of unparallel happiness rather than of a few moments of unbearable agony. But life is not a bed of roses for any of us. Events usually gain up on us and catch us off guard. Fortunately, we had a happy ending. The whole process that all three of us went through to get to the happy ending may have been hurtful but it brought us all closer together.

Actually, coming to think about it, now I will have ammunition for sending my daughter on guilt trips when she will be a teenager and will no longer listen to us. When she becomes all rebellious and acts irresponsibly, I will tell her:

— You should be ashamed of yourself, treating us like this…are you forgetting that when you were still in the womb you scared us to death? …we ran around panicked all over Athens to visit the best doctors to see if you were OK… and this is the "thank you"?...is that what I expected of my daughter?....

Did that freak you out? Do you have memories of your parents scorning you in a similar way? Or even worse, do you remember yourself talking to your kids like that? What can parents do? Sometimes, when they are desperate or feel that they are not on top of the game, they may have to resort to such measures.

They don't mean it, believe me. I would do anything to make sure my girl is all right and I haven't even seen her, I haven't even held her in my arms yet. I found the strength to do it and I would find more if I had to. Where from? From the endless power source that was mentioned before, the Babysource!

All Mighty Babysource, I say a prayer to you,
I ask of you to give me strength,
I ask of you to give me patience,
I plead that you give me knowledge,

To care for my baby, to love my child,
To stay up at night, to feed and clean it,
To be creative and inventive of solutions when I am
ignorant and weak,
All Mighty Babysource, show me the way,
To keep the diaper on, to warm the milk right,
To smell the flowers in my baby's poop,
To laugh when it pees on me,
To smile when it pukes on me,
Last but not least All Mighty Babysource,
I ask of you to be endless, now and forever!

October 26ᵗʰ, 2010   Week 24

Rena is back from Athens and the whole family is back together again. Our home is about to return to its normal routine. In the morning, I am the first one to leave for work after I pick up my brother-in-law Makis and after I feed, water and pet Loulou, our dog. An hour later, Rena and my father-in-law will follow after they also feed, water and pet Zena, my father-in-law's dog, a beautiful and very clever German shepherd. My mother-in-law stays home, as a happy retiree, and takes care of all the house issues as well as her elderly mother who lives with us. She will take care of the parrot and will have an argument with her mother, for breakfast, and then they will love each other again. In the afternoon we all get back from work, first Rena and her father and then I follow. Rena waits for me to get back for lunch and then we take our afternoon nap before or after our usual bed chats (our bed has become a strategic headquarter of important decisions). In the early evening I get up to take Loulou for a walk while my father-in-law takes care of the chickens and walks his dog, Zena. We may go downtown for chores or shopping. And that is the rhythm of our quiet three-storied home, inhabited by three generations… or rather four if we include the imminent baby girl!

During our afternoon bed chat today:

- Yiannis, I don't like it when you are away…all these days that I was in Athens I didn't like it that you weren't there, too.
- I know, baby, but there was nothing we could do. What are you going to do when you leave in the middle of December to stay in Athens till you go into labor? You must start getting used to me not being around all the time.
- I know, but I don't have to like it. You know at night, when I laid down, I talked to the baby about you.
- You did?
- Yes!
- And what did you tell her?;
- Stuff…!
- Like?
- Well, you know, stuff, about you being away, how good you are and other stuff…!

She didn't want to tell me what she was telling our daughter about me but just the fact that my two girls were talking about me while I was far from them makes me want to strut like a peacock. I am not sure what it is that makes me feel like this, maybe the idea that people need me and I mean things to them. Why seek social and professional recognition from strangers when in your own home the most important people in your life miss you and talk about you? That's recognition and good reason to be proud. That is success and that is happiness!

October 27ᵗʰ, 2010

Isn't it strange when aspects of your character unfold in given moments but without expecting it? There are well-hidden behaviors that you don't allow to manifest because you find them wrong but sometimes they jump out of your subconscious just like that, simply and primitively.

Today Rena called me at work and told me that she wanted to stop by the office to wait for me to finish work. She wanted to go shopping for the baby to pick out some more things. Initially, I had no problem with it. She often comes to the office and waits for me to leave together. When I hung up, though, I had second thoughts and something made me pick up the phone again:

Rena, actually, don't come by the office! It is better for you to ask your dad to take you after you both finish from the hospital.

- All right, but why? Are you busy?
- No, it's not that, I mean, I am busy, but it's not that.
- Then what?
- Well, I don't want you coming here with your pregnant tummy and have everyone come up to you and tell you stuff. I am not sure everyone has the right intentions. I don't want any talk… you know!
- I got it! No problem! Don't worry, I'll go with dad.

I was scared of the evil eye today. Usually, I don't pay attention to such superstitions and I have even made fun of them at times. But at work, I can count in one hand the people that I know that honestly mean well. It would be unfair and paranoid to say that the rest don't mean well but we don't all have the most pure and honest relationships. After all, in a workplace, you can't get along with every single colleague, it is impossible. When it does happen, it is most likely superficial and led by common interest. Many times you are forced to compromise and maintain some formularized business relationships, after some initial bickering, in order to get the work done. That is what we are there for, to work and produce. I would rather not think like that and not be so cynical but I was gradually made to do so, people and situations made me.

So, I didn't want to subject my wife to indifferent comments by some. Like I said, I am not superstitious but when it comes to the well-being of my girls who come in an attractive 2 in 1 package, I will be downright superstitious and everything!

November 2010

November 1st, 2010   Week 25

This afternoon our little one gave it her best again in Rena's belly, reminding us of her presence and her good health.

- – This afternoon the little one was very active again.
- – Really? I wonder why!
- – Who knows? But I managed to calm her down.
- – How?
- – I was stroking my stomach and I talked to her.
- – What did you say?

From what she told me, I imagine that the dialogue between the fetus and the mother went something like this:

- Come on my girl, take it easy. I guess you are uncomfortable in there and you have nothing to do.
- Right cross punch with a light header (Translation: if you were cooped up in a sack with indeterminable liquids and no light, what would you do?)
- Be patient for a few weeks. You just make sure that you are well and that your heart is well and you will see how much fun it will be when you come out.
- Left uppercut and half a turn counterclockwise (Translation: Really? What kind of fun?)
- You will have your own room which we will decorate with nice colors. We will go for walks with your pram and I will buy you pretty clothes.
- Right kick and change of position (Translation: clothes are nice mummy, thank you, but can I get some toys, too?)
- Your dad will get you toys and grandma and grandpa will be so crazy about you that they will fulfill your every wish.
- No response from the belly (translation: ahhh nice…I am tired now…I will take a little nap… wake me in the evening for a snack, ok?...i love you mummy!)
- All set baby? Good girl!...get some sleep now…I love you very much!

November 5th, 2010

Getting towards the end of the sixth month, Rena's

stomach has become a big round ball that changes shapes according to the moods and movements of the baby. We think that at this point we can tell where the baby's head is because we sometimes see a bump on a specific place on her stomach which is always harder due to the muscles being pushed outwards.

As new and exciting as all this may be, the fact remains that Rena is carrying a little human being who is growing and she has started feeling "heavy". She can't sit in one place for too long whether it is the sofa or a chair. Even in the bed which is the most comfortable of all she keeps having to change positions and sides. She becomes tired more easily and she gets out of breath even more easily. Her back aches more often than before and some nights the pains in her back in combination with the exercise program that our little athlete follows keep her awake. The doctor told us that the best way to deal with the back pains is walking which we have also noticed that it works.

At Rena's work at the hospital, they are very understanding of her condition and they make sure not to tire her much. Nevertheless, the hours at work and the thirty-minute ride to and from the hospital wear her out. She has noticed that every time she rides in the car for a long time, her stomach hardens and she swells up. The house chores are now completely inaccessible to her. I help out as much as time allows me and we hire a lady more often to clean the house. We have been using the same lady the past years because she is very good at what she does. Dust is her sworn enemy which must be defeated and driven far away. When we enter the house after she has cleaned it, it feels like a whole cleaning crew has gone through it and not just one person. There is a smell and sense of cleanliness that makes her a champion. We had tried others but she is by far the best.

Last night, oddly enough, we both dreamt of our baby. Rena dreams about her more often but last night both of us did.

I dreamt that I was waiting outside the room that Rena was in labor in. Then, Rena opened the door and I saw the nurses bathing a very strong and active baby with long light brown hair. I didn't see her face very well, mostly her back. Only for a moment did I catch a glimpse of her and she resembled me. I am obviously affected by my father-in-law and Rena's brother who saw a three-dimensional sonogram of the face of the baby and, although the placenta was stuck on her little face and it wasn't so clear, they immediately commented on the resemblance to me. She can take after me, too, but I really wish that she inherits her mother's beautiful eyes and lips!

Rena had a very clear dream of her face. She had round blue eyes. The chances of her having blue eyes are very limited since only very few people in both our families have had blue eyes. Rena also dreamt of light brown hair. That is quite likely to happen because both of us have the same skin tone and hair color, we are both light in skin tones, I have brown hair and Rena has light brown hair. Actually, my hair is starting to blend in some grey but not so much that one couldn't discern the original color.

We shall see…!

November 6ᵗʰ, 2010

"Oh!...Well, don't worry, maybe the next one!"

This was the response we got from a distant uncle of Rena's when we told him that the baby is a girl and not a boy as he would apparently be satisfied with. We were at the grocery store and the scene was played out in front of the store's employee who knows us well.

- Hello uncle, how are you?
- Hey…kids…How are you? I didn't see you standing behind me.
- How are you doing? How is the aunt?
- We are all doing great! Wow, I see you are getting bigger. I guess the little guy is growing.
- It is growing all right…and growing well…but it is not a little guy, it is a little girl.
- Oh!...Well, don't worry, maybe the next one!

We were just standing there with our mouths open that someone, in 2010, had the audacity to say something like that to us. Even the lady at the cash register was embarrassed to hear that and felt awkward being there. I have to admit that I wasn't so surprised. You expect to hear comments like that from elderly Greeks. They were raised with such a mentality, one that we will never be able to understand, let alone, justify.

Nowadays, things change at such a quick pace that it is impossible not to have huge generation gaps. In very few areas of Greece, you can still find people who when they say the word "child", they mean boy. If, for example, someone has two daughters and a son, when asked if he has any children, he will answer "I have one child and two girls". In the older days, having boys was considered great luck while the more girls that were born in the family the more the burdens. Surely this way of thinking stemmed from the fact that only the sons worked outside of the house and were the sole providers of income while the daughters stayed home until they got married without working and contributing, financially, at least. The men were stronger and more capable of working the fields. But even back then this way of thinking was counterbalanced by arguments from the other side that it is good luck to have a girl born in the family due to the care of the household and of the members that she could provide. A black and white film from those days included a very indicative scene.

The plot was about a Minister who was visiting villages in the Greek countryside because elections were coming up. He wanted to get back in touch with his voters in order to secure his re-election. In one of the villages that he had to stay due to a technical failure of his car, a pregnant lady was assigned to welcome him and show him generous hospitality. In one of the scenes, they show this lady talking to her mother-in-law and expressing her concerns about how her husband is going to react if the baby is a girl and not a boy. One would expect the mother-in-law to support her son's preference to have a boy. On the contrary, she replied: "What do you mean, what is he going to do? What can he do? Nothing! Can anyone argue with God's wishes? He is going to love her, just like your father loved you, just like my father loved me. After all, if no girls are born, who is going to have the boys?". The effort of the screenwriter to pass along the right message, even in those days, was simple and effective.

The social and economical circumstances that could justify this prejudice are understandable but…enough is enough! I have had it up to my neck with this shit.

The next person who will dare shoot out a similar comment in front of us is going to have to deal with a furious father-to-be. Wake up you poor, miserable, petty little people, those of you who say stuff like that, and realize that every child is a blessing and the more negativity you pass on to a child, the more chances it has of becoming like poor, miserable you. Don't you wish to see a better world? Don't you want to see a world in which the people that are raised are better than you and not clones of you?

That should be the goal. If you let the years go by without grasping the cosmic changes that are happening all over around you, that is your problem to solve and your issue to deal with. Who gives you the right, you ignorant fool, to transfer your long lost dignity as a man to a little girl? What gives you the right, you loser, to take your incompetency to become the man you wanted to be and compare it to a little girl to make you feel better? Do you by any chance think that by degrading women you will win points in the ladder of manhood? If so, you are fooled. All you are is a sample of a man who never understood the greatness and the diversity of women and, of course, the woman who is by your side all these years must be just as stupid as you are, otherwise how would she tolerate a bonehead like yourself?

The differences between men and women don't separate us in different army camps. A smart General would take the pluses from both sexes and would fight better forming one army, not two. The differences between men and women don't separate us, they just define us.

November 7th, 2010

November is in and my fellow about-to-be dad-friend that I met in Kiev is waiting for his son to pop out any day now. I called him today not knowing if I will find him at home or at the hospital. He was home; the little guy is still not out. Vassilis and I were joking while in Kiev about the fact that one day our kids could get married.

All the members of the Kiev delegation were invited to the Greek ambassador's house for dinner. So all six of us got into a van and took off for the formal evening. Our driver, Anatolis from Kiev, was driving too fast so I asked one of the ladies that was with us to ask him to slow down, not that she spoke Ukrainian, she was just sitting closer to him.

– Could you ask Anatolis to take it easy cause I will be a father in a few months and I want to be in all pieces, whole, when my child comes?

Vassilis didn't know that we were expecting.

– Come on now, are you also expecting? Us too!
– When?
– Mid November.
– Really, you guys are close. What are you having?
– A boy.
– A boy, eh? Well, let's shake on it; we will get those two married!

Everyone at the van burst in laughter and Anatolis was looking at us through his mirror, probably thinking we were weird and loud.

– With pleasure, we will have your girl and we will become in-laws.
– Yes, but how are you holding up? Never mind, I don't know you well enough to ask you such things directly. I don't want to ruin the matchmaking. I will ask around Samos about what sort of assets you have.
– You will, won't you?
– Yeah, that's right! Of course, you should keep in mind that you are not the only suitor, many boys are waiting to come out around the same time as my girl and there are some others with

a nice age difference of a year or two, so the grooms are many!

The rest of the colleagues in the van were following our exchange and were waiting for the next funny line, to scare Anatolis once again.

Back to today, Vassilis told me on the phone that the doctor told them that they should be on guard. He is a travel agent and this season is not peak season for his business so he has a lot of free time to devote to his wife. When I wished him well for the labor, his response sent out signals of fear and concern.

- The labor is going to be fine. What happens next, Yiannis, at home?
- Are you scared for the first days at home?
- Well, yeah, it is our first time, what are we going to do?
- Listen, from other fathers that I have spoken to, they tell me that you don't have time to think much. The baby needs constant attention during the first days so the care alone will run things for you. You know what I mean? Everything is going to snowball on its own. Don't worry, you will do fine!

Vassilis was definitely on the end of the line but I get the feeling that I was telling him things that I wanted to hear!

November 13th, 2010   Week 26

Rena's hormones, as well as mine, are going nuts these days. We have both become very emotional and sensitive to anything that has to do with babies. On TV, especially on diaper commercials and toy commercials, the babies and the children who star in them are carefully selected to generate feelings of motherhood and fatherhood to us, unsuspecting viewers. The moms, or the future moms, who watch them see these chubby, huge-eyed angels and they think "What a sweet baby, so cute!" or "What a mischievous little guy he is!". The fathers think "Look at that little princess, I will gladly empty my wallet for her" or "What a strapping little guy, that's how mine is going to be and we will do all kinds of sports together". The advertising executives know what they are doing. They know how to tap our most inner instincts of child making and parental care.

On the other hand, I don't want to put all the blame on the advertising companies because how hard is it to get moved when you see a beautiful baby even on the street! Not at all hard! Just take a walk in the afternoon and you will see parents pushing the strollers with their bundles of joy inside, fathers playing with their kids at the playgrounds, mothers holding them by the hand, those who are old enough to walk. You will stop and look inside the stroller, at the playgrounds you will watch the children run around and play in the sandpits and climb those colorful metal structures like monkeys and, always with the parent's permission, you will start up a conversation with a 4-year-old who you think is cute and spirited.

These days we have been concerned about a couple we know who are facing a serious issue with their pregnancy. She is in the seventh month and she has frequent bleeding. She has placenta detachment and she must be very careful not to be too active. One doctor has alarmed her and another has reassured her that there is no serious problem. We are troubled by the fact that the one doctor is telling her that she has nothing to worry about. How do you know what to do when you have such difference in opinions? I hope they stay cool and wise and I hope that the optimist doctor is right.

When Rena told me their story, my first reaction was to hug her with one arm and put my other arm on her stomach. It was as if I was protecting her from the story she was telling me, as if hugging her could protect her and our daughter from similar incidents. If I could become a shield and fight off anything bad away from Rena and the baby, I would definitely do it.

We both felt sad about our friends. I don't know about Rena but I also felt guilty because I was greatly relieved that my wife and my daughter are in perfect health compared to our friends. Anyway, everything is going to be all right for them and their baby girl will be fine and, who knows, their daughter and ours may be best friends.

The other day Rena and I were watching an older movie with Geena Davis, a movie that really touched our hearts. I don't remember the title and it doesn't matter. The film was set in my favorite city, New York. She got pregnant by her fiancée but she finally decided not to marry him because they were not compatible. So she decided to have the baby and raise it herself with the help of her parents. When the child was born, his one hand was deformed and he had some health issues that didn't allow him to breastfeed. The mother, being very emotional from everything that went wrong and thinking that her little guy rejected her, left the baby to her father and set off to a quest to find not only herself but also her mother who had also abandoned her. After she managed to find her mother and face the ghosts of her past, she regretted leaving her baby and went back to New York to start being his mother. The baby was in the hospital suffering from pneumonia. She stayed by his side day and night.

While the baby was intubated in the incubator, his

mother looked around to make sure that no nurse was watching her. She carefully opened the incubator, took his little hand and started talking to him. She told him that she knew that she had abandoned him and that he had every right to be angry with her and not want to wake up. Why wake up if he was going to have a mother who doesn't want him? She reassured him that she will be there for him and that she will never let anyone hurt him. Then she asked him to wake up and give her one more chance to love him.

Unreal! The mother was asking her baby to give her a chance to love him, a chance to raise it and care for it. That baby, or any baby in the real world that has parents that think like that, is very very lucky. Any parent who realizes that raising a child is a privilege more for the parent than for the child is going to raise a stable, balanced person. When a mother or a father reach such levels of deep consciousness of what they are doing and what they have to gain from raising a child and if everyone who took on the responsibility of raising a little angel thought this way…I am going to say it although it is a cliché…the world would be a better place!

November 14th, 2010

Today is election Sunday and I woke up early in the morning as always. I got up quickly, too, because I didn't want to think. When I wake up in the weekends and I have the time to stay in bed, I usually stress out about all those things that trouble me; I can't get them off my mind and relax. So, I prefer to get up and start getting busy with things that will distract me. I know that I exaggerate in my concerns and that sooner or later everything gets taken care of.

My problem today was not what I would vote, I already knew that, I had decided days before. I was stressing over my financials, always in connection with the baby's arrival. I still need to save up 2.000 or 3.000 euros for the private room at the hospital. I have to pay 2.500 euros to the Revenue Service by the end of the month (this doesn't have to do with the baby) and come up with 1.000 euros to pay for all the baby's things when our order arrives. Everything will be taken care of eventually, with proper planning. I just sometimes let my financial obligations get me down, but not for too long. I am thankful to have Rena who always calms me down by telling me that the ten years that we have been together not once have we not been able to settle our debts.

In the late evening we watched the election results for a while and it seems that the mayor in Thessaloniki (the second biggest city in Greece, up north) is going to be Mr Yiannis Boutaris. Even though I am not from Thessaloniki, this gives me double pleasure. The one reason is because I know his son very well through work and I respect him immensely. The second reason I am glad is because when Mr. Boutaris expressed freely some of his ideas and opinions about church issues, the Archbishop publically asked him to take back what he said, otherwise he would make sure that he is not elected Mayor. This priest thought wise to let all of us know that he can control things in the political life and obviously thinks that he is powerful enough to affect Mr. Boutaris' election as Mayor. I suggest that he occupies his time with the religion issues and with the teachings of Christ, teachings of love and humility.

Irritated by the above, I told Rena:

– See? Boutaris was elected. The priest didn't manage to stop him.
– The whole incident probably worked to his favour.

– Definitely! Can you believe the nerve of this guy to come out and say what he said? Next time we go to church I will only offer 1 cent for the candle. That will teach them church officials!
– Come on now Yiannis what does our little church have to do with all that? We support our church and its maintenance.
– But the money we donate goes to the big heads.
– That can't be true! How is the church maintained?
– I don't care! I am not donating another cent. They should go out among us and teach love instead of threatening and blackmailing. They are out of control! No more donating!
– Yiannis, that is not right.

And she went on to say, jokingly:

– ….and you should know I am going to tell our little girl what you are saying!

I thought about it for a while, I got angry, and I said:

– Go ahead! I don't care!

It is three of us; already it is three of us! I realized that because of the way I felt when Rena told me that she is going to tell on me to our girl. The idea of my girl criticizing me about not donating any money to the church bothered me and made me feel awkward. I could almost see her in front of me, looking at me frowned and with her little hands on her waist telling me::

143

>   — Daddy, that's not right, not to give money to light the candle for little Jesus!

And how can I make her understand where I am coming from? At that young age she wouldn't.

I must arm myself. Mother and daughter are going to know how to push my buttons and manipulate me. They will find what pisses me off and what makes me soft and they will use it against me.

That's all right! Sweet tyranny!

November 18th, 2010

A few nights ago, the baby was hyperactive and Rena got very little sleep. She kept switching sides to calm down the little one but it didn't work. The exercise and development program was intense that night. Naturally, Rena was dragging the next day. I was in deep sleep all night long and didn't sense what was going on. She felt sorry for me and didn't wake me to keep her company.

The following night we were afraid we were going to have a repetition of the previous one, so Rena was proactive and had a chamomile. She had noticed that whenever she had soup or something warm in liquid form, the baby became very quiet. The trick worked. Both my girls slept all night long without interruptions.

Driving from work today I was thinking about my wife's ordeal and I was wondering if she was angry or at least irritated with the baby who hadn't let her sleep that night. It wouldn't be unreasonable to be irritated since she couldn't sleep. The lack of sleep alone causes agitation, let alone when there is a specific cause that you can be agitated at. Typing these lines now, I hear a voice behind me, the voice of an experienced parent, smiling sarcastically and saying: "My poor man, you think that is hard? During the first weeks your little angel will wake up every little while and you will be getting very little sleep on a daily basis". I choose to ignore the voice and I continue….

-   Rena, can I ask you something?;
-   Yes.
-   The other day that the baby didn't let you sleep all night…were you mad?;
-   What?
-   Were you mad? Did you get irritated with her?
-   No…what is she supposed to do? She is closed in there and she had to do her little exercises.

Rena was very beautiful and very cute the way she was defending her unborn child.

-   I love you Rena! You know why?
-   Why?
-   I love you because you love our baby!

November 21st, 2010

On Sundays I usually find time to read my magazine and that is what I did this morning. I buy this magazine almost every month. It addresses the man of today with mostly health and exercise issues. This month I bought it because one of the articles advertised on its cover drew my attention and excited my curiosity.

The article is the confession of a man who persistently supports his right to not want to be a father. I was thrilled when I saw the article's topic and I really wanted to read this man's story. I definitely do not agree with him but I find it very honest of him to openly admit that he is not made to be a father. It is preferable to accept the fact that you don't like children or you don't want to raise children, rather than be forced to do it due to social pressures.

This man, the self-called non-father, explains the pressures he is under from his social circle to accept the fact that eventually he has to have a child. His mother is pressuring him in her own way and he is starting to feel the same pressure from his girlfriend. Even though his girlfriend is well aware of his beliefs about wedding and children, he understands himself that at some point she is going to want to have children and join the club of happy parents. I laughed when I read that his mother is trying to convince him by telling him that one day he is going to be a great dad. He writes that to be able to remain a non-father requires a lot of effort on his part especially as the years go by and he gets older.

The non-father prefers to focus on other things. He must be successful at his job and have a decent income to be able to maintain a lifestyle that includes travelling, fine dining and women. A conscious non-father sees kids on the beach pulling on their father to play with them and make sand castles with them while he enjoys his peace and quiet bathing in the sun with a pretty lady on his side who has an awesome body since she has never had a child before. This man dreads the idea of being surrounded by hyperactive children who were born to suck out all his energy and all his hard-earned money.

Reading this article I was glad to see that there are people who realize the responsibility and the emotional commitment required to raise a child and consciously choose to keep their distance from this role. If they feel that they can not cope or do not want to cope, then that is their God-given right. This is preferable to making a kid miserable by being forced into having it and raising it. I imagine that men who think this way have also thought of the consequences of their choices. I mean that they must have accepted the fact that when they get older, they won't really have family to take care of them or care about them because this lifestyle choice is usually accompanied by the lack of a steady partner and close relatives.

I didn't expect the course of the article after his avid declaration of non-fatherhood. At a friend's house he was given to hold his girlfriend's godson. Ever since, the baby has become inexplicably attached to him and a very strong relationship has been formed between them, something that of course shook our hero's beliefs. The non-father and his new mini friend became inseparable. They played together, he fed him, read him stories, took him for walks and many more. It was clear that the writer of this article had changed.

The question is whether he had changed because it was the right time for him to change or he had just finally given in, even if it was subconscious, to the pressures of the people around him. Maybe he had matured and maybe along with maturity comes the need for reproduction. Or maybe he just got tired of everyone expecting him to become a dad and he decided to test himself by allowing himself to get attached to the little guy.

Maybe it is the magical innocence of a small child and the privilege of being shown love and being chosen as its friend that can change the life of the most cynical and scared person.

November 26th, 2010   Week 28

Till now I have not written anything about my godsons, I have two. The one is George who I baptized when I was only about 14. He is now a young man who I see rarely, unfortunately. I have missed many of his years growing up because I was away in Canada studying and for the longest time we had lost touch. We now talk over the phone but only two to three times a year. He is always very nice to me but we don't have the relationship that we should have had. And it is my fault, exclusively mine. I feel guilty about all those years that we've missed and about the fact that someone else bought him his Easter candle because his godfather was always away. I think I deliberately avoid meeting him when I visit Athens for business. I can't get over the fact of my being absent from his life and his presence constantly reminds me of that. I must get over it, though, and try to at least become friends with him. I promise him to try and I hope that he wants me to make such a promise, if he is still interested.

My second godson is Stefanos. He is the son of a good friend of mine for who I stood in his wedding as his best man. He is about three and something now and he is also far from me, in the city of Korinthos, an hour away from Athens. Having learned from my first experience with George, when I was asked to become the godfather of their child, I told them to think about it very well because we would be far from them and I wouldn't be able to see the kid as much as I would want to and as much as they would want me to. With me being in Samos our contact is not easily facilitated since living on an island so far away means that I am dependent on the weather and the minimal ship routes that our good government has taken care for us to have. And when the ship takes 8 to 10 hours to get to Athens, you think twice before you do the trip. The alternative is to spend a small fortune and take the plane. Thank God for Skype! At least with Stefanos we communicate with the help of technology every or every other Sunday. The courier companies are also an important part of our relationship since most of the presents we have bought him have been delivered by someone in a uniform.

Stefanos' mother is pregnant again! When Stefanos was told of the good news and realized that he is going to have a sibling, he asked his mother for a little girl. He wanted to have a sister and the reason was his parents' goddaughter. He was disappointed though because the first sonogram showed that the new member is going to be a boy, too. He compromised; he accepted it and he went on with his carefree life filled with his cars, his bulldozers and his swords.

Somebody up there, however, decided to do him the favor. I received an e-mail today from his mother:

"…I hope our daughters become good friends!..."

The first sonogram tricked the doctor and our friends. It's a girl. Stefanos' wish will come true after all. My young godson knew better than everyone, even better than the medical equipment. If only his wishes always came true like that in his life, so easily and so magically!

November 27ᵗʰ, 2010

"My dear baby girl,

I feel the need to write to you again and give you only a brief description of the world that we are bringing you into in a few moths.

Things are not easy. They are easier than other times but they are still hard. You will be born in a world which can be wonderful and very rough at the same time and sometimes horrid. We people have the ability for great good but also for terrible evil and I am not telling you things that are new, everybody knows it. It is just that when you actually write it down, you start accepting it and you don't go mad.

We have daily proof that we are much worse than the rest of nature's animals. Having the mental capabilities that we do makes us special and this is something good and useful and something that evolves us. But sometimes the way we use our brains enlists us in the most brutal beings on the planet. Our power for love is the same as our power for destruction. You will find out yourself growing up, unfortunately!

You will be born in a Greece that is going through very difficult times. Years, or rather, decades of corruption and abuse of the public money have brought us to a desperate situation where our country is forced to live on loans which will never be able to repay. Whose fault is that, they say? It is our own and especially the Greek politicians'. Greek politicians were the ones who wasted and misused financial resources of this country, especially those resources that were given to us for funding and for the community's benefit. Greek politicians were the ones who decided to put themselves, their disgusting, slimy selves, above the interest of those people that they were supposed to be serving.

You know what, no! I refuse to take any responsibility for what is happening to my country. However, I am called upon to save it with my own blood and sweat. My baby girl, they have been trying to convince us, they who have brought us to the edge, that it is our fault, the citizens' fault. I refuse to take any responsibility for this chaos because I have been working since 19; because my parents worked hard to provide us with an education and to leave us with an important legacy. Because nothing was given to me for free and I had to fight to earn any little thing.

I am not ashamed to be Greek and you shouldn't either. However, I am ashamed about what they have done to us. I am ashamed about the rotten Greeks who always find a way to get into the government. You know how they do it? They are lazy by nature. We, the hard working and conscientious citizens, occupy most of our time with our work and spend most of our time doing it right. They haven't learned and never wanted to work a day in their lives and they have no idea what it is like to create and produce. Therefore, they destroy instead of structure. They seek positions of high power in the government of this once-upon-a-time proud country so that they never have to work hard again. They only work hard until they get them. They get educated, trained, they promise unrealistic utopias to the voters and once they reach their goal, they start destroying.

Your mother and I are thinking of leaving Greece. We want to get away from all this corruption and ugliness. We are not cowards; don't even think about that, not even for a moment. We are just tired of working for people who don't deserve us. They are trying to pass on the message of patriotism and convince us to stay in Greece these difficult days. But they don't deserve us! We and you deserve better treatment, a more dignified treatment. And, really, we should consider ourselves lucky. We haven't lost our jobs, at least not yet.

I have thought of relocating to New York many times. I love New York, my baby! It is the most alive city that I have ever visited. When you grow up, we will all go there together and I will show you why I love it so much. I also like London, and it is much closer. London is also an amazing city which has a lot to give to anyone who knows how to receive it.

My good baby, the world can be very beautiful, too. In this world you should strive to live, in any way and geography given. Nature is fascinating once you explore it. The creations of man can enchant you just as much as a dreamy, magical sunset. You can find joy in small things and bigger things. With us you will learn to love to travel, to see new places, to enjoy a gourmet dish accompanied by a carefully-selected glass of wine, to buy beautiful clothes and unique things, to mix with interesting people who have a zest for life, to love yourself and the people around you.

One thing is for sure, my darling! We will show you both sides of this world that we are bringing you into and we will teach you how to survive choosing to live on its beautiful side. Even more certain is that this world will be more beautiful because you will be living in it.

We are expecting you…!!

With lots and lots of love!
Your father"

December 2010

December 12th, 2010   Week 30

*I*t seems that when I wrote my second letter to my baby, I vented so effectively that I didn't feel the need to write again until today. There were many things that preoccupied me for a long time, not just me, all Greeks. Many young residents of this beautiful but troubled country have been thinking of relocating abroad because all they see in their future is dead ends. Anyway, no matter what happens we will fight, we will survive, we will cope.

Lately, Rena has been having pains in the bones of her pelvis. She can feel her bones opening. To me, that sounds very painful and freaky but it is a necessary process that prepares her body for labour. She usually gets these pains when she is lying in bed and they last for a few hours. Then they go away and come back after a few days. She read in her book yesterday that this indeed happens to some women and is not easily diagnosed by the doctors.

She has also complained to me about heartburns which

she didn't have before. They say that when a pregnant woman has heartburns it means that the baby is growing hair. We will check the book for that, too.

I wish there was some way that I could share these bodily changes with Rena, but there isn't. I feel guilty that she has to endure everything herself. When she says to me that her pelvis bones are actually opening, I feel useless and insignificant. I am not saying that I don't want her telling me these things or that any pregnant woman shouldn't open up to the father of her child. Of course, we fathers must join in this process, this game of creating life. It is preferable for us to get goose bumps listening to all these changes that their bodies are going through, even if there is nothing we can do about it, than not knowing and not being included. To me, ignorance and lack of involvement is much worse. Therefore, I declare myself to be an involved husband and father. I don't know whether this is a valid term in psychology or not but I responsibly declare my participation and involvement, even if it is only emotional.

December 13th, 2010

My new friend, the one I met in Kiev, the prospective in-law, has indeed become a father. He now has his first child, a son. I called him today to see how he is doing. I am always apprehensive to call on the phone people who have a newborn at home. You never know when your call is going to disturb them. What I worry about the most is not to wake the baby especially if they have just managed to put it to sleep. And it is even worse if they have lied down to take a much needed nap and the phones start ringing like crazy.

I called him on his cell and I found him in his office.

– Hey Yiannis, how are you?
– I am fine, how are you with the new little guy in the house?
– We are very well but, you know, very tired also. Last night, for example, we stayed up almost all night because the baby had pains and was crying. He sleeps only for a short while and then he wakes up again.
– How are you feeling?
– It is an incredible feeling, the best in the world, no doubt about it! However, there is some tension in the house and I just found a window of opportunity to come to the office to see what's going on here. Last time I was here was 3 days ago. I will clear my head a bit and then go back home.
– How is your wife?
– Overall, she's fine. She is a little overwhelmed, a little irritated from the lack of sleep, but fine.
– Do you change the baby at all?
– Are you serious? From the first week. My wife was hesitant to handle the baby in the beginning, so I took over. I just dove into it and I learnt. You should do that from the very beginning. Don't get intimidated! Just dive in!
– That's what I was thinking of doing from the very beginning too. I am planning on starting to handle the baby straight away and not let her tiny size scare me off. I mean, if others can do it, why not me?
– Exactly my friend, you do just that! Call me you guys for a coffee (the other guy is a guy who works in the chamber of commerce and we have become good friends cause he is as crazy as I

am). Don't forget about me now that I have become a dad and have to stay in all the time.
– No problem, we will call you! Kisses to my son-in-law!

The size of a newborn is something that always intimidated me. They are so small and fragile that the idea of holding them terrifies me. I imagine that this is my chance to get over it. Now, with my own baby, I should become an expert. I am resolved not to let myself chicken out in the sight of such a fragile creature. I know that her little head will need support. I know that I must not touch the top of her head while she is still very young although Rena told me that we may have to softly massage a certain way the bones of her skull to help it shape up properly. I will let my wife-doctor do that. I know that if I want her to bond with me faster, I should hold her naked from the waist up so that she can come in direct contact with my skin and learn my smell.

As far as the changing of the diaper is concerned, I am going to become a champion! The right preparation is going to play a critical role here. The way I imagine it, we must have all the right "equipment" available at any given time in order for the de-shitting to take place quickly and efficiently. I must know where to lay the baby once I take off the diaper and where to dispose of the diaper immediately and I must have all the necessary stuff next to me. Tissues, towels, powders, I don't know what else, I guess they will show us at the maternity ward. I must speak to the baby throughout the whole process and tell her stories or even talk to her about what I am doing to her. This will help my movements become mechanical and I won't make the baby feel nervous, as I will be feeling. Remember, babies sense everything! At this vulnerable age, the instincts as to the emotional state of the people around them are highly developed. It is a defense mechanism given to them by nature since they are unable to react and communicate. So, when you open up the color-changed diaper and you are faced with a little pile of your treasure's waste, display composure and play it cool. "So what? To me, that's nothing! You think you can scare me with that? I don't think so!"

December 12ᵗʰ, 2010

The time is getting closer and our fears are starting to surface. Up till now, anything related to the pregnancy seemed new and exciting. Shopping for the baby is fun, talking about it all the time and making plans is just as fun. It is fascinating to imagine the baby at an older age, making its first steps, playing, saying its first words.

But now that we are only a few weeks away from the desired event, you can sense a sweet anticipation and fear for the unknown in the air. Rena is afraid of the labor. She is afraid of the pain that she is going to feel if, for some reason, they don't get to do the epidural anesthesia. She is afraid of the prospect of a caesarian section. She is afraid for the baby itself because there are several different things that could go wrong and harm the baby during labor. Her fears are absolutely reasonable and I am glad that she expresses them to me. The first thing that I can do is bow before women for the ordeal their bodies undergo and the second thing I can do is give my wife a big hug and whisper in her ear that everything is going to be fine.

I am terrified, too, though! I am not going to talk about the birth process and the dangers that the mother and the baby are under because the idea of something going wrong scares the living daylights out of me and I simply don't want to think about it. My concerns focus more on the first days, the first two months. I am wondering if we will be able to care for our baby the way we should and the way she deserves. Actually, I used the wrong pronoun when I wrote "we". I should have written "I". I am positive that my Rena will know what to do; I have complete trust in her. It is mostly me I am worried about. I don't know if I will be able to identify when our little one is hungry, when she is sick, when she will have colic pains, when she needs to be changed, to be bathed, when we must change her diet and many more.

Knowledge is power! Rena reads and gets informed on a daily basis. I have to sit myself down and read this book we bought for the first year of the child. I have started it but I am only in the beginning. I think that now I am ready to go on and finish reading it. The need for that is pressing, my inner self demands it.

December 16th, 2010

When I came back home from work today, I followed my usual routine. I walked in the house, called out "hello darling" to Rena who is always in bed at that time resting and watching TV, I took off my shoes and clothes and I drooled over the food that was waiting for me on the table, wonderfully prepared by my caring wife. She cooks most of the time now because she started her pregnancy leave. I walked in the bedroom, kissed Rena, gave a gentle stroke to the Belly and I headed towards the kitchen table to tame my hunger.

Rena got up and came towards me telling me: "Are you so hungry that you didn't notice anything?" She pointed towards the couch where I was surprised to see three pink sleepsuits with elaborate designs on them. All three had been purposely laid on the back of the couch. These were my little girl's first clothes!

- What are those?
- Sleepsuits for the baby. Mom and I went shopping today and got them. They were on sale!
- Look at them, they are so cute...so funny!.
- Aren't they beautiful?
- Very! So, the baby will get in there?
- Yes!

Her first little clothes, the first of many! These are the first garments of the fruit of our love. These little suits will keep her warm and protected from external conditions. When she wears them, they will be clean and freshly-washed and she will feel warm and secure. These clothes will be part of our daily life and of our family. These are not simple pieces of cloth sewn together, they are something else, they are her first clothes. Never before have I ever loved baby clothes so much!

After I soothed the beast in my stomach after a hard day's work, I took the baby's suits from the couch, along with the hangers, and brought them with me in bed. I covered myself and I put all three of them between Rena and me on top of the comforter. I looked at them, I looked at them again, I handled them, I opened all the buttons and buttoned them up again. I "studied" them well. Then I hugged them and fell asleep...

December 18th, 2010

We have entered the 8th month and, according to the doctor's orders, no more trips for Rena, that is, Rena won't be able to be going back and forth to Athens any more for the doctors' visits and the ultrasound exams.

Today is Rena's settling in Athens. So we took the ship yesterday from Samos and here we are in Moschato, Athens. We obviously took a double cabin in order for the mother of my child to lie back comfortably and sleep quietly. She needs to be able to change sides all the time, according to the tastes of my demanding, capricious daughter. We have also taken along the car, which I am going to leave in Athens in order to be able to get around, especially closer to the dates of the expected labor. The total cost for the one-way trip to Athens, tickets for two people and a car, 280 euros! For God's sake and this is for 8 hours in a boat…anyway!

The action plan follows:

Rena will stay in Athens until March 7th. We are expecting around February 15th. On March 5th one of her cousins is getting married in Athens, so we will stay for the wedding and after that, we are back to Samos. I will stay in Athens from today until January 3rd when I will be replaced by my mother-in-law and I will go back to Samos for my work. I may come up for a few days in January but for sure I will go back to Athens on February 7th for three weeks, one week before the labor, the week of and one week after. Then I will go back to Samos for a few days and then I will finally go get my family and bring them back to the island. For as long as I am not with Rena, her mother will be with her or my parents or some other relative here in Athens.

I am so worn out! I had to load the car yesterday which was a great test for my edged out nerves. You have to be a wizard to fit into one car the things that I managed to. There was no room for Rena. I had to load things even on the passenger seat. Rena had to be taken to the port by her dad and in Athens from the port to home by her uncle. The worst of all was that at the end of the loading I had to fit in the last two suitcases which I had to leave for the end. I had planned room for them in the trunk on top of two carpets. So I went to the car carrying both suitcases, opened the trunk and something was telling me that it was not going to close. I was right! At that very moment the good God decided to send a cloud over the island and it started raining hard. Picture it! An open trunk, two suitcases on the ground, two carpets folded in square shape in plastic bags also on the ground, and a furious about-to-be dad standing in the rain, soaked, and wondering why it had to start raining at the most critical part of the loading. And I was cursing…! Not someone in particular…just cursing! Eventually, the All Mighty felt sorry for me and enlightened me as to a way to re-arrange everything and make the trunk close. When I unloaded everything today, a whole day later, the suitcases and the carpets were still wet.

The chores in Athens are many, extremely many! For today, all we did was buy a Christmas tree and decorated it to get into the mood, here in Athens, too. Next year, there will be three of us decorating, not two. As of today my Christmas leave begins and as of tomorrow the chores and the shopping for the baby's coming commences. I am worn out! Goodnight, I am too tired to care if the bedbugs bite!

December 20th, 2010   *Week 32*

Today's ultrasound exam was very short, luckily! Everything seems normal. The baby is 1.800 grams, a good weight for the 8th month; she is neither thin nor fat. Congrats to my wife who shows great self-restraint and follows a very balanced and healthy diet. Not that she is my wife, but she is the most beautiful pregnant woman I have seen. I tell her that but she doesn't believe me. She has maintained a good enough weight for the baby to receive the quality and quantity of nutrients she needs and look chic and elegant at the same time. If you see her from her back side, you cannot tell she is pregnant. So far, she has only gained 6,5 kilos. This month, though, she must start eating more because the baby needs a daily intake of 800 calories!

Coming back to the sonogram, the doctor showed us a three dimensional picture of the baby. She was sleeping in that shot and her eyes were shut. This was the first time that we had seen such a clear picture of her face. I guess my father-in-law and the others were right when they said that she looks a lot like me. I started seeing it today, too. The doctor said the same thing. She looked at the baby, then at me and said: "She looks a lot like her dad!" I hope the female version of me is good. In the male version, I am all right, I am not Brad but I am presentable. Let's see how I turn out in female.

December 23rd, 2010

Finding the baby's cot is not an easy task, at least not for me and Rena. We always like to find things that are special and not at all commonplace. We enjoy making a difference with our choices, with things that we find whether it is clothes or furniture. We make sure, if we can, that there is something different about them. This sometimes means that we have to pay more but in some cases less. In this case with the cot, less!

Our baby's cot is wooden and it is all white with no designs or colors. It has narrow bars on its left and right side and wider bars on the top and bottom side. On all four corners it has four bed posts that rise to the ceiling and with a mosquito-net they create a dreamy little bed with canopy. Its style is simple, minimal and romantic. The one side is adjustable as is the mattress which means that it can be used as a little bed till the age of five, maybe even more. After that, it can be turned into a little sofa.

They delivered it this afternoon and we set it up. It was in pieces. It is a good thing that it included very detailed instructions and all the necessary tools. As I was putting it together, I caught myself singing Christmas songs. I have put together furniture of this type before, the ones you can set up yourself and with only a few tools and good instructions you feel like a talented craftsman. But never before have I enjoyed it this much. Time flew by without me realizing it. I was extra careful not to make a mistake and have to start all over again. I was especially careful not to forget a screw or some kind of supporting piece and run the risk of the cot dismantling while the baby is inside. As I was working on it, I felt that I was doing something really important for our child. I was in charge of making the bed in which my daughter is going to have fairytale dreams filled with fairies and butterflies, beautiful colors and magical stories backed by harmonious melodies that will soothe her and take her to lands far away.

I put together the big pieces in the living room and when all of them individually were ready, I moved them to the bedroom to set them up in the place we had decided it was going to go. I did have some technical difficulties there because two people were needed to fit in the two sides of the cot and to make sure that they screw into each other firmly and safely. Rena helped me as much as she could by lightly holding them and balancing them. We did it! The cot-bed was ready in its place.

Before we threw over the mosquito net, we had to decorate the walls that it was adjacent to in order to create a colorful corner. Of the many cartoon characters that exist, our favorite for our little girl is Strawberry Shortcake. She is a cute girl always dressed in brightly-colored clothes, clothes that refer to a child and not girly clothes that refer to adult women. We really hate dolls or cartoons that project an image much more feminine and way sexier than they should for little girls. A young girl is a small child and not a miniature of an adult woman. A grown woman has the right to choose clothes that accentuate her sexuality, a young girl doesn't even know what "sexuality" means and she doesn't need to until her puberty. Therefore, the role models that surround her must correspond to her age and maturity level.

Strawberry Shortcake is a darling little cutie pie. She is always smiling and she wears bright clothes and a big hat with a strawberry on it. When our baby wakes up and is able to focus her eyes on the wall, she will see a little story. She is at the countryside and is taking a walk. The sun is shining and there are very few and sparse clouds, just enough to define the sky line. She will also see trees, green grass, a few small butterflies flying about, a smiling caterpillar and a frilly ladybug.

When we finished decorating the wall, we threw the mosquito net over it and from the side that we will pick up the baby we opened it up by tying each side to its corresponding post with a pretty bow. It is a very romantic picture. We also put the changer next to the cot. Ready! Then we sat on the bed across from it hugging and gazing at our baby's first bedroom. We think that we have created a safe, soothing environment for our baby's first days. We both agreed that it looked so relaxing that we wouldn't mind taking a nap in there!

December 25th , 2010

Merry Christmas! These are the second Christmas that find me writing this diary. How different things were in my life last year on the same day!

Christmas is always a bitter sweet experience for me. I've always had very happy Christmas as a child and as an adult. I can't recall an unpleasant event taking place during Christmas, something that could have traumatized me. On the contrary! I have many happy moments to remember. As a child, what I remember most is decorating the Christmas tree. We had a huge, fake tree that we set up every year. It reached all the way up to the ceiling and it was very wide. At least, that's how it seemed to me. After we had it standing tall and placed in a corner in the living room, we would open the boxes with the ornaments and the decorating would begin. I remember many ornaments in many different colors, red and golden garlands, pieces of cotton loosely scattered on the branches to resemble snow. As we used the same tree every year, in my eyes, it was almost a member of the family. Honestly, I was really fond of it.

As a grown-up, the most special Christmas was two years ago. It was the Christmas that Rena and I spent in Paris. The weather was cold; we were walking the streets of Paris enjoying the sights both of us bundled up in our scarves and our caps. About every two hours we stopped wandering and warmed up our cold, tired bodies with warm coffee and profiterole or some other sweet masterpiece made only as the French know how.

We spent Christmas day at Disneyland! The magic was everywhere, abundantly generous. It was a childhood dream of mine to visit Disneyland and I am glad I got to do it with Rena. We stayed there all day; we arrived at 9 am and left at 8 pm. The cold was sharp but it was worth it. We had no idea that on that very day Disneyland had its 15-year birthday anniversary. A ceremony was organized after the Christmas parade and it was absolutely spectacular. You had to have had more than two eyes all around your head to be able to catch everything that was happening around you. Snow was gently falling and all the Disney cartoon characters were up on a stage singing. One by one got on stage to start performing and you could hear in many different languages of the world exclamatory comments such as: "Look, it's Mickey and Mini", "Wow! There comes Donald!". The highlight of the ceremony and the closing at the same time was the illumination of the castle of Sleeping Beauty. It was filled with thousands and thousands of colorful lights and they kept interchanging. We stood frozen still watching with our mouths open. We had become children again, two children holding hands and thinking how much fun our children are going to have when we take them there one day.

The bitter part of Christmas is owed to the distance between the blessed family moments that we have and the moments of loneliness that some other people have, especially children. I am not concerned about those children whose families don't have a lot of money but for those who don't have a lot of love. I can't stop thinking of those children who spend Christmas in hospital wards with little boxes of medicine to keep them company. Amazing how the world's injustices fall upon the souls of such children! But remembering about these children and weeping about their bad fortune is not enough. We must all do something about it. I have never really done much, nothing that makes a difference anyway. The only thing that I have done is jot down my feelings about these children in this diary and hope that others who read it, if it ever gets published, get motivated. However, others, who are less hypocritical than me and more heroic than any war hero, have given up their time and parts of their soul for such children.

At the S.O.S. villages here in Greece, children who have been abandoned or taken away from dangerous, unhealthy home environments are raised by "mothers" or "big brothers" who help them regain their dignity. Others have used their fame and fortune to build hospitals for sick children. These people are the Santa Clauses of the world and I wish that one day God will consider me worthy enough to help me join forces with them in order to contribute; in order to have the privilege to contribute.

December 26th, 2010

Dear fellow about-to-be dads,

Do you know where the hospital where you wife will be giving birth is? Have you driven there at least twice and at different hours of the day so that you know with what kind of traffic you will be faced? Have you found alternative routes in case one of the roads is closed or there are road works going on? Do you know exactly where the entrance for your wife who is in the car dilating in pain is? Have you saved the doctor's contact numbers in your cell phone and in a physical agenda (cell number, the office's number, the home phone number, his/her mother's number and, finally, the phone number of the convenient store across his/her house)? Have you saved in your cell the hospital's number and the number of the midwife, if you hire one?

If you haven't done so already, think of the following scenario. Your wife's water breaks or the labor pains are starting. Panic is in the air! She takes her hospital bag, which she has so carefully prepared days before, and looks at you straight in the eyes and expects of you to transfer her to the hospital quickly and safely. You get in the car and you realize that you are not exactly sure of how to get to the hospital, only roughly. You fall into traffic, you roll down the window and start asking strangers for directions, you miss the exit and you urgently need to find the way back, you start cursing at the government for the insufficient road signage (you will be right but it is pointless) and, worst of all, you run the risk of getting into an accident because your attention is not on the road. You don't even want to think about the possibility of delivering your own baby in the car because you are incapable of finding the hospital. OK, you won't have to pay the doctor his/her enormous fee but, think of the car seats…! When and if you finally arrive, you realize two things. Your wife is looking at you wanting to tell you that after you get home with the baby she is filing for divorce and you have completely forgotten to notify the doctor who is going to need almost as much time as you did to get to the hospital.

Following is the ideal scenario. The contractions have started or the water breaks and your wife informs you. You, as an impeccably organized husband, tell her in a charming and calm manner, the manner of a man who knows how to deal with emergency situations effectively, "No problem my love! You get ready while I notify the doctor and the midwife to meet us at the hospital. We will be out of here in 5 minutes and in about 13 minutes we will be at the entrance of the hospital". It is certain that she will be thinking "Oh God, what a man!" and she will not regret it, not even for a moment, that she selected you to father her child. .

So, prepare, prepare, prepare!

December 28th, 2010

The last couple of weeks we have been faced with several dilemmas; important decisions about the labor, our baby, our life.

Dilemma no. 1: Which hospital should we have our baby at?

Our doctor works with two hospitals. The one is well established and reputable with experienced staff and reasonable prices. The downside is that it is far from where we will be staying. In the unlikely event of clear roads with no traffic, we can be there in 30 minutes. In the most probable case of heavy traffic in the streets of Athens, who knows when you will get there? That scared us and got us thinking of another alternative. The possibility of Rena's water breaking during heavy traffic hours and us being stuck in the car while her contractions become closer and closer is terrifying and out of the question. On the other hand, if we didn't have another option, we would either leave it to luck or schedule the labor.

The second hospital is brand new and only a 7-minute drive from the house. The downside was the prices. They asked for 400 Euros more, in total. The amount was not that much considering how close it is to us and how convenient it was going to be. I had already started favoring this option but I thought it would be wiser to visit it in the inside too and talk to someone before we finalized our decision. Due to my work, I am used to negotiating frequently and I was hoping to manage to reduce the price. Times are tough to pay extra.

Parking is a bit tough around the hospital but they have a special entrance for emergency entries. On the inside, it is very shiny and luxurious and it smells "new"; bright marble floors, employees dressed in perfectly ironed uniforms and smiling faces are the first things you see when you go through the main entrance. As I mentioned, it has just opened and the efforts to attract customers are apparently intense. The clean-cut gentleman and the lovely ladies at the reception sent us to the first floor at Accounting to be informed about the prices. This was the moment my negotiation skills would shine, or so I thought. How could

I negotiate when we were standing behind a counter and the lady from Accounting was talking to us behind a clear glass? My bargaining power was diminished by the fixtures. The way I had imagined it, since we were interested in a single room thus more expensive, was that we would be talking to a customer service person in an office in a more private situation. In the office, I would talk to them about their competition and try to convince them that they need to reduce prices in order to attract people. The least that I would ask them for would be to give us equivalent prices to our first alternative. But the setting was not appropriate for negotiations. However, my brilliant wife thought to ask if they have special discounts for doctors. The lady's answer lifted a huge weight off my shoulders.

– Of course, you have 30% discount!

"How much?", I reacted thinking that my ears are playing tricks on me and that darling lady repeated the number. I asked her to make a note of it on the price list and we left the Accounting department happy to have finally selected the maternity clinic. The final price is much cheaper than our first option.

After that, they suggested that we were taken to the top floor to see some single rooms. They wanted to "lock" the sale by showing us the facilities in which we will live those unique in our life moments. Passing through the hallways we saw the registry where you register the birth of the baby and where they inform you about the process you must go through in order to notify the state that it just acquired a new little tax payer. What impressed me the most, though, is the fact that there is a bank branch in the hospital, not an ATM machine that you can withdraw money from but an actual branch with employees and cashiers and the lot.

After the baby is born and the parents are ready to take the discharge, they go to the bank which is on the same floor as the accounting department, they pay, take the proof deposit slip and then turn around and hand over the deposit slip to accounting. I just hope that the services that we pay for are just as efficient as the system they have established for the payment (or draining as I could call it but my upbringing prevents me from doing so).

Dilemma no. 2: Which company should we choose to store the stem cells from the umbilical cord of our child?

Medical science has advanced so immensely that it gives parents the option to store the stem cells from the umbilical cord of their child into private banks. In case the child gets sick with a serious disease related to the blood like leukemia, anemia (lack of red blood cells) and certain diseases where the body attacks its own cells, the so-called autoimmune diseases, then you can request the stored stem cells for the doctor to use in the therapy. It is a significant cost for the parents but not unattainable. An average price for a 20-year storage is 1.900 Euros. These private banks offer discounts in the form of immediate payment incentives but they also give you the option for monthly installments. This is money that you pay and wish that you never have to get what you paid for.

We interviewed three companies, one Greek and two foreign ones with offices in Greece. We weighed the advantages and disadvantages of each and we decided. The procedure is quite simple. You notify the company that you have chosen before the time comes and they send you the "box" which contains all the necessary instruments and receptacles that the doctor will use to collect the sample. The box must always be next to the bag that the mother-to-be will take with her to the hospital for obvious reasons, not to be left at home. The collection of the sample takes place right after the baby is born. Once the sample is collected, you call the company and they come and pick it up themselves from the hospital. They immediately send it to the labs where the sample is tested and if it hasn't been compromised, it gets stored. They send you the test results along with the invoice, of course. By then, you have already paid an advance and at this point you are asked to pay the rest either in full or by monthly instalments, usually three. In case the sample gets rejected due to an infection or some other form of unsuitability, it gets destroyed and you don't have to pay any more than the advance you already have, for the costs up until that point.

It is certainly an issue which a parent must at least look into and get informed about. Usually, doctors recommend such companies but it would be useful for parents-to-be to look into it on their own also and talk to different banks to get a better overall picture.

Dilemma no. 3: Should we move as a result of a job proposal?

I was fortunate enough to be offered a position from a winery whose owner I admire and respect deeply. He has been in the wine business since he can remember himself and he is one of the best professionals I have ever met. He is open-minded and always two steps ahead of all of the rest of us. He has the exquisite gift of knowing how to listen to people who talk to him and to pay special attention to each and every one. He wins you over from the first five minutes that you have a conversation with him and he generously passes on his knowledge in a very discreet way. For a long time I had been thinking that if I had to change employers, I would want him to be the next one.

The position has excellent potential and a better pay. It would be a great challenge for me to take on the exports of the specific winery. The fact alone that this man was very positive about a potential cooperation between us for a position that up until now he hasn't trusted anyone else but himself to fill is a great honor for me. The downside would be that I would have to be away from home often as I would have to live separately from my wife and child for the first couple of years. Rena would have to stay in Samos for another 2,5 years until she finishes her training at the hospital and I would live in Athens and would have to fly out every weekend to see them. I am intensely troubled by this but if I accepted the position, I could get the week's work all done in four days and I could fly to Samos Friday morning. The position would require me to have a laptop with me at all times, anyway, and a lot of the work would get done outside the office.

It is a sacrifice that as a family we may have to make because the money is going to be really good and it would be very fortunate for us to be able to increase our income at a time of crisis. Besides the money, my career would skyrocket and I would be considered to be among the most significant executives in the wine business in Greece. At least, this is how I see it. I am positive that this move would open up new professional and social horizons for me and my family. It is certain that Rena and our daughter would benefit also in the long run.

What I have to think about, though, is how I will be able to spend quality time with my child, this child whose coming we have been anticipating for so long. I had imagined that I would spend a lot of time with her. Children are too young to grasp concepts like "career" and "potential", children just want their mommy and their daddy. Even though many children have been raised normally with long temporary absences of their parents, I am still very skeptical to make such a move. In Rena's family, her mother had to be away for a year as she had been appointed to work at the island of Rhodes. She took the plane every weekend to be with her children who were raised by their father and grandmother. Even in my family, although I saw my father only for a couple of hours every day, due to his heavy workload, I still adore him and I consider him my guide in many important decisions I have made in my life. I am getting carried away, though, and I am forming scenarios in my head. I sometimes do that because it helps me sort things out. Nothing is certain yet! After all, I am quite pleased where I work now and I am not sure that I would accept when and if the proposal became more specific.

January 2011

January 1st, 2011   Week 33

*H*appy New Year! Happy and Healthy new Year to all!.

Happy New Year to us and our families! This is going to be a special year for us. The emotions we will experience will be new and unique! The first moment we will lay eyes on our baby girl, the first awkward efforts to hold her, our inexperience as to her care and the first smiles that she will give us to compensate us for the long sleepless nights. The first presents, the joy that the baby will bring to the grandparents and the uncles!

Happy New Year to our friends, to those who are still looking for their soul mate, to those who have found it, to those who have already had their first child.   Happy New Year to our friends, to our dear friends who have not been able to conceive yet, unfortunately, and are so unjustly hurting! I can't write about the latest developments of the couples that are still trying, I think in vain. It is too painful for me because our prayers and wishes don't seem to matter anymore. Happy New Year beloved friends, armed with patience and optimism!

January 2ⁿᵈ, 2011

Many of the new mothers that we have been talking to lately are vouching that the midwife they had hired for the labor and the breastfeeding really helped them out a lot. We talked to our doctor about it and he encouraged us to talk to a midwife to see how we feel about the whole thing. He suggested that if Rena felt positive about it after she talks to her, we should go ahead and hire her. He referred us to the midwife he had used for his wife. The cost for the services of a midwife ranges from 300 to 500 Euros depending on the services that will be agreed on. .

Oddly enough, the meeting was arranged for today at 11 am. Even though it is Sunday today and the second day of the year, she agreed to see us because I insisted to see her, too. I am leaving for Samos tomorrow and since she couldn't make it last week, we picked today to get together and meet.

When I called the midwife to arrange the meeting, the truth is that she thought it was really strange that I called her and not Rena.

- I would rather talk to your wife.
- Of course you will talk to her; I am only calling you to arrange the meeting.
- But it's her that I am going to be talking to anyway.
- Yes, but I will be there for the meeting, too. I want to meet you and be informed also about the process and your services.
- Will you be in the room during labor?

–   I really want to but we want to hear what you
    have to say. And if I am in the room, I need to
    know what to expect, right?
–   Right…you are right. Ok then, have your wife
    call me later so that we can figure out a day and
    time that is convenient to all of us.

It seemed a bit odd to me that an experienced midwife
like her insinuated that the relationship between a midwife
and a woman expecting is a relationship from which the
husband should keep his distance. Maybe she is not used to
talking to fathers about such issues or maybe not too many
fathers get involved in the process. How was she to know
that she was on the phone with a self-called participative
father who dives in without any hesitation? Besides me,
Rena wanted me to be there at the first meeting with her so
that we can exchange opinions about her later. I was really
glad that Rena asked me to be present at this meeting. The
idea of the guidance of an inexperienced pregnant woman
from an experienced midwife who is also possibly a mother
is extremely threatening to a man. A man feels useless
and powerless when faced with the deep knowledge of the
midwife and the trust shown to her by the mother during
those painful moments. I guess that a man feels as ignorant
in this case as ignorant a woman may feel in front of a father-
son discussion about sex and women.

The meeting was realized and the midwife came with
only a few minutes delay since it was raining outside and
she had to walk from the train station. I offered to pick
her up from the station but she preferred to benefit from
the exercise. "She is my kind of people!", I thought. She
was very giving with Rena when she walked in. She met
her for the first time and while she greeted me with a plain
but firm handshake, she hugged Rena and kissed her on

both cheeks. You just don't kiss someone on both cheeks when you meet them for the first time. In my eyes, this emotionally generous behavior of hers was the breaking down of Rena's defenses. It was as if she was telling her: "Trust me! I don't know you and you don't know me but with me you will spend some of the most thrilling moments of your life. Let yourself trust me!" This display towards Rena was a clear message to me, too. It was as if she was telling me: "Good for you that you are present. But what you planted in so much pleasure, I will bring into this world through pain and blood."

I sat at the kitchen table with them but on the opposite side far from them. I didn't talk much. I only asked about what I couldn't understand and I let them bond. I was as respectful as the situation demanded. The midwife talked to us about when, how, and under which circumstances we would go to the hospital. She described what happens when we get there, procedure-wise, what happens in the preparation room and the delivery room. Rena kept asking questions and the midwife replied in a calm, sweet, soothing manner. We both hang on her every word. Halfway through the meeting she started addressing me also and I guess that was my first victory, my first step into getting included.

When she started talking about the baby and its care after it is born, the way she narrated, softly and motherly, and the mental images she was creating made me start getting choked up. She was so detailed about how the baby will come out and how they will place in on Rena's nipple. They didn't see me silently crying. They were so absorbed by their conversation. Although initially I had thought that this midwife is a bit rigid and old fashioned, during the meeting I could hardly restrain myself from getting up and giving her a big hug, being grateful that she was in our house and devoting her time to us.

Our meeting lasted for about an hour and a half. When it was over, our midwife showed Rena how to push when the time comes, and we set our next appointment for the hospital, when the time comes. She encouraged us to call her any time for any questions we might have and then she asked me to get her coat, another indirect way of showing me my rightful place. She said goodbye to Rena in the same warm way she had greeted her. She turned to me and extended her arm for a cold goodbye handshake. This was my chance to break down the wall that she was putting up between me and her, between the unsuspecting, ignorant, male sperm donor and the wise, high priestess of child birth. I extended my arm too, gave her a handshake and before she had a chance to pull her arm back, I pulled her towards me, kissed her on both cheeks and gave her a big, bear-like, thank-you-for-taking-care-of-us hug.

We both loved her!

January 3ʳᵈ, 2011

I am on the boat returning to Samos. My mother-in-law flew in to Athens from Samos with the morning flight and we changed guard. The next scheduled date for me to go to Athens is February 4ᵗʰ.and I will stay on till labor. I hope I don't have to fly in earlier because that would mean that two things will have happened. Rena's grandmother, who is living with us, may face a serious health issue which, in turn, means that Rena's mother will have to fly back to Samos to take care of her. Or Rena could go into labor earlier than expected if our baby decides to join us ahead of time.

Rena was a bit upset the previous days with my upcoming departure. But it is unavoidable since we decided that we are better off having the baby in an Athens hospital. I couldn't take any more leave for now because I had been away for too long. It is rare for me to be able to take more than two consecutive weeks time off. .

When I left this morning, I hugged my wife, I kissed her and then I leaned down to the Belly and I told my baby girl that I love her very much and I kindly asked her not to pop out till I come back.

January 7ᵗʰ, 2011

Today is my name's day (St. John the Baptist day) and it is one of the very few times that I am spending it alone, I mean, without Rena. It could be the first time, I can't remember well. I was compensated though because I received many gifts apart from the many telephone calls and e-mails for wishes.

The "gifts" are not exactly mine but my baby girl's. I had her things delivered today, her pram, her rest seat and the cradle. The cradle, a reminder for the inexperienced fathers, is a miniature cot in which the baby sleeps when it is still an infant and for a few months later. It is small and it fits in the parent's bedroom. Everything delivered in the afternoon. In the evening I occupied myself with the pram-pushchair system. This versatile vehicle promises many hours of entertaining and moving the baby around. Depending on the baby's age, it changes shapes and forms so that the baby can be comfortable in relation to its development. It is perfect! I set it up twice on my own and then I took it downstairs to demonstrate its functions to my father-in-law and aunt Maritsa who was over to help us out a bit, being two bachelors me and him. So, the pram is ready, I will "study" the rest in the following days.

I feel better today! I am relieved that the baby's things arrived so that I learn how to use them. I am also relieved because I managed to save up the 1.200 Euros that they cost and I was able to pay for them. Tonight, I am going to sleep peaceful and happy that I can take care of my family!

January 10th, 2011

The previous days were tough. On Saturday, Rena's grandmother fell and broke her hip. She was out in the garden taking her usual walk, slightly irritated that her daughter is away to Athens, and she tripped and fell to the ground. We took her to the hospital where she was diagnosed with a broken hip. The surgery was arranged for today and my Rena's mother took the first flight from Athens.

My mother-in-law's arrival to Samos means that Rena is in Athens alone. Of course, Maria, her cousin and best friend has been recruited and has already moved in her stuff and staying with her. She will be the one looking after my pregnant wife for a while.

Naturally, I got stressed! Rena is in Athens, without us, getting bigger, and her mother and I are in Samos having no idea when she is going to go into labor. The only good thing is that everything has already been arranged with the hospital, the doctor and the midwife. My parents have been notified of the situation too to keep a close eye on her. Tomorrow at the office I have to focus 100% on my work and wrap up all my pending issues so that I will be able to leave when my wife and unborn child need me; although I have the feeling that they need me now and I am away. What should I do? How did things turn out like this? This is not a good time for surprises and unexpected events.

January 11ᵗʰ, 2011

I can't stop thinking about today's daily goodnight call with Rena. Rena is very concerned, I can tell from the tone of her voice. She is feeling insecure and it is so reasonable.

–   Yiannis, I feel strange, I feel my body changing day to day. I talked to my aunts about these signs and they told me that I might be going into labor soon. Make sure one of you arranges to come up; otherwise I think I am going to give birth without you.

I have to leave! I will arrange everything at work tomorrow and I will book a seat on the evening flight to Athens. I have to leave…!

January 12ᵗʰ, 2011 *Week 35*

Tonight I am writing from Athens. I went to work in the morning and I started settling all the issues, preparing my colleagues in my department for my absence and schedule the following weeks. The employees in my department have supported me a lot whenever I needed it and I have done the same for them. We always count on each other and we make sure that the absence of one of us does not interfere with the department's proper daily functions. In this way, no one ever loses face.

The uncomfortable part would be to inform the General Manager of my sudden leave. That is not how we had planned things. We had arranged for me to take the leave 3 weeks in February, not now. January would be the preparation month for my absence in February. Fortunately, I have been preparing since December and I have been organizing things since then in fear of something like this happening and my having to leave. After all, I have the laptop with me and I can follow and coordinate issues from afar. I even take my laptop with me when I am on leave or vacation and I always find time to check my e-mails and send instructions to my people at the department. This is not professional addiction but it is the nature of my position. I don't have to do it but if I didn't, in the long term, it would have a bad reflection on the company and on me. All these years that I have been working as a Sales Manager, I have made sure never to get accused of unreliability or lack of professionalism or indifference towards my clients. I have only benefited from this behavior so far and I will in the future. Doors are wide open for me and that is a good feeling.

The manager was informed, I went home in the afternoon, packed my suitcase, took the baby's car seat and my father-in-law drove me to the airport. My in-laws' relief was evident. They didn't feel right that things turned out this way and we had to leave Rena in Athens with relatives, even for a few days. I am sure that when I told them that I am leaving for Athens on such short notice, I became a small hero in their eyes. But nothing heroic happened. What happened was the obvious and the given for our families. That is how we do things in both of our families. We all support each other. After all, how could I hear my wife's voice like that and not rush close to her?

When I arrived in Moschato, Rena's embrace was warm and firm. A pregnant woman is very vulnerable, both physically and emotionally. She constantly needs to feel safe and loved. She needs to know that there is a whole support system behind her to understand what she is going through and to take care of things to perfection when the blessed time comes. Some men may think that I am exaggerating and they could say to me:

> – Easy buddy! It is not just your wife that is having a child; so many others have and so many others will!

Correct! But life is too short to let individually unique moments like these pass by lightly. The miracle of conception that took place between Rena and me and the even greater miracle that has been taking place in the Belly all these months now have filled my soul and heart exactly because I am living and enjoying every single moment. .

After I unpacked my suitcase and had a coffee to recover from the tension of the day, we went to the doctor. He told us that we should be expecting the baby in January and it is very probable to welcome her in the next 7 to 8 days. Our feelings when we left his office…joy and fear…combined!

January 13ᵗʰ, 2011

The signs of labor, those that made the doctor tell us that we may be having the baby sooner than expected, are different from woman to woman. Rena has the following: her lower back is hurting, she feels a burning sensation in her sensitive area, she is sleepy all the time again, just like she was in the beginning of her term, her chest is not swollen anymore, she has preparatory contractions and extra vaginal secretions. According to the guidebook that Rena has been reading, we are approaching the desired event. Rena's mother was informed and she is preparing to fly up on Saturday. I hope she gets here on time.

Since the doctor told us to expect her very soon, I assume that she is going to come any day now or any hour now. This is why I have already prepared my own hospital bag. I will stay with Rena in the single room so I must have my own things that are necessary to make my stay comfortable also.

The happy father's hospital bag should contain a pair of pajamas, slippers, 2 long-sleeved T-shirts for comfort, an extra pair of jeans, a nicer outfit for the nicer pictures that will be taken when we leave the maternity ward, underwear and shaving gear. The most basic of all is camera and video camera for obvious reasons. I will also have the laptop with me so that I can load the pictures of the baby. Since the visitors will not be allowed to get close to the baby, we will show our impatient friends and relatives the pictures from the computer. My internet stick will also seem very useful for communicating with the outside world although I don't know if we will want to get away from our world filled with our angel and its care.

January 16th, 2011

It is Sunday today and it's three of us now in the house of Moschato; my mother-in-law flew in yesterday.

All this waiting has made me think thoughts that I decided to share with Rena during our afternoon rest.

- Rena, have you realized how many years we have been together?
- Yes, eleven….it sounds unreal, doesn't it?
- Incredibly unreal! And what is more unreal is to think where we were then and where we are now.
- When we met, I hadn't even graduated medical school.
- And now you are about to become a mother… amazing!
- I am a little worried.

– About?
– I am afraid I am going to get postnatal depression. It happens to many women.
– I don't think you will get the baby blues because you are already very attached to the baby. My explanation may not be scientific but I feel that you are prepared to welcome our little one and you know very well what lies ahead regarding her care. I mean that I don't think you have the wrong perception of what is going to happen after the birth and you will not be caught off guard by the exhaustion and the responsibility. You are already talking to her and you don't consider her as something foreign to you. You two have already bonded incredibly and all that is left is for her to come out of you so that you can continue on your relationship. I don't think you will be like other women who look at their child and don't completely realize that it is theirs, that it is part of them, a piece of them.
– I hope you are right.

Today Rena had contractions, long ones every hour and short ones every fifteen minutes. This lasted for four hours. We are scheduled to see the doctor on Wednesday but we will probably go tomorrow to have him check for any developments.

January 19th, 2011

On Monday we went to the doctor's, I guess mostly due to my impatience, and he sent us for an ultrasound exam today. Everything went very well and the doctor confirmed that our baby girl is doing fine. She hasn't progressed enough, however, not enough to expect her as soon as we are expecting her.

Not having much to tell us, the doctor kept showing us her face on the three dimensional sonogram. She seemed very beautiful to us and we got very excited when we saw her make a strange face pouting her lips and when we saw her taking amniotic fluid out of her mouth in bubbles. The doctor gave us the cd so that we can watch her at home too and show it to everyone and anyone who drops by, of course.

January 20th, 2011   Week 36

- Rena, today is the 20th, it's the date that the doctor had told us that we might have been having the baby.
- Yes, but she is not ready to come out yet. What can the doctor do? With all the symptoms that I have been having, it is only logical for him to expect me to go into labor soon.
- There is nothing else to do but wait.
- We will wait, that's for sure, but, Yiannis, I am tired!
- I understand, you are right to be tired.
- I don't sleep well at nights, I feel very heavy… come on baby, come out already so we can see you!
- Yes, she is going to come out and we will have her with us to take care of her and the two of you will be the best of friends!
- I love you Yiannis!
- Me too!
- You know why?
- Why?

- — Because you are the father of my child.
- — Only for that?
- — No, but for that also. Whatever happens in the future between us I will always love you, at least only for that.
- — You won't have to love me only for that because we will always be together ok?
- — Ok!

January 27ᵗʰ, 2011

Our baby girl has deceived all of us; she has her own opinion of when she will come out. We were expecting her a week ago, earlier than scheduled, but she seems to have gotten quite comfortable in the Belly. The doctor had told us that she has progressed a lot and is in position, so all we had to wait for was the water to break or the labor pains to begin to get in the car for the long-awaited route to the hospital.

To be perfectly honest, this constant waiting has irritated us. Rena is irritated because she wants to stop feeling so big. She has contractions that won't let her relax. They are creating the illusion that we are approaching and we are constantly on guard. Every time she has one, or consecutive ones to be more precise, an imaginary list unfolds in my brain which is burnt by now with all the organizing that needs to be done. It is physically exhausting for Rena and psychologically exhausting for me. My absence from work also troubles me because I can't be sure what is being talked about by the people who have the right to talk about my being away from work all these days.

And let's not forget grandpa, Rena's father, who is still not a grandpa but he is waiting all on his own in Samos. My parents call us every day to see how we are doing but al least they are together. My father-in-law is alone on the island waiting. He is also anxious about being able to jump on the first plane to fly to Athens to be here for his daughter. What plans does he have in his head for his first grandchild I wonder? What plans are my parents making about their third granddaughter? I wonder if they have the same anxiety and enthusiasm that they had for their previous grandchildren or the fact that they now have a deeper knowledge of being grandpa and grandma has made them more cool about it.

Returning to the Belly, let me mention that it has descended quite a bit and the mother of my child sometimes feels that our angel is just going to slip out. She gets that feeling mainly during our daily evening walks. Walking helps open up the cervix.

Tomorrow we are visiting the doctor...urgently... again!

January 28ᵗʰ, 2011

We didn't have to go to the doctor after all. We told him the signs over the phone and he told us that we should be expecting to go into labor during the weekend. He preferred not to see Rena because he felt that if he went looking down there he might induce labor interfering in the course that Rena's body and the baby have taken.

February 2011

February 1ˢᵗ, 2011   *Week 38*

$\mathcal{F}$ollowing is Rena's letter to our baby:

"My baby girl,

Some time ago, your father asked me to write you a few lines for the diary that he is making for you but only now, a few days before we see you, did I feel the need to do so. I say "before we see you" because to me you were born 7 months ago when I first heard your little heart beating inside me.

Up until 7 months ago I was a woman who enjoyed the independence and excitement my job had to offer me. I became a doctor through many hardships and sacrifices and be sure that from a very young age you will also learn how important it is to get an education and to be able to count on yourself. This is what I want to offer you as your mother, the love and foundation you need to be able to stand on your own two feet when necessary.

During the last months, my world as I knew it till I got pregnant with you changed. Ever since I found out that you are inside me, I stopped breathing for one and I started breathing for two. I felt what it is like to be responsible for someone else and that filled me with happiness, not fear; except for some moments that I got scared about your health. Those moments seemed like ages and I will never forget them and if I hadn't had your father to share my agony and pain, to be comforted in his arms, I would have caved in.

I am proud of two things in my life. The first thing is that I managed to create something so perfect as yourself. The second is that I provided for you the best protector and guide in the whole world, your father. As you grow and get to know him, you will understand what I mean and why I love him so much. Ever since he entered my life, about 11 years ago, I learned how beautiful it is to be loved and how much more beautiful it is to love. Only when you give love can you receive it and absolutely feel it. These and many other feelings that you can't still understand my little girl I have had the happiness of sharing with your father 11 years now. And lately we have been sharing the miracle of your creation. Love him, my little girl, because you are his whole life and because there is no other man that deserves it more than he does

In a few days we will hold you in our arms and your magical journey in our world will begin. I hope I have offered you a good home the past months. I hope you will manage to love us despite our mistakes that we will surely make because, after all, my little daughter, we are now a family and family members love each other not because a law defines it but because that's how it is, because you are blood from our blood.

Welcome our baby girl!"

February 4th, 2011

On the first of the month I left Athens to return to the office for a while, back in Samos. Although I was able to work from afar all these days that I was gone, I had started felling uncomfortable about being away for so long. Now that I am returning to Athens, today Friday afternoon, my conscience is clear.

Sitting at the airport waiting for the boarding announcement, I am looking forward to seeing my wife. I missed her, even if I was away from her for four days, four days that the doctor gave me "permission" to leave. Now I know that in 3 days we are entering the last week of the 9th month, we are entering the final stretch at the end of which a darling, vulnerable angel will be waiting for us to bless us with its grace and the miracle of its existence.

I am looking forward to seeing the woman that wrote this amazing letter to her daughter and who honored me so much with her words. I feel so complete being with her, content and safe! I feel safe that she loves me so much!

February 8th, 2011   *Week 39*

Following is an e-mail I wrote to an ex-colleague and now friend. She called to find out how we are doing:

"Good Morning,

Thank you for thinking of us and calling us to see how we are doing. I am always glad to hear that you are well and that things are going well with your new job.

You got me thinking yesterday when we talked and I felt the need to write you the following. You may feel strange about what you are going to read or you may feel that we don't know each other that well but I think our friendship is growing, I am really glad about that by the way, and I will come out and tell you.

A few years ago, I was as passionate about my first child being a boy as you are about your first being a girl. However, things happened to some friends and relatives of mine that made me reconsider. I had to reconsider, not the preference of sex but my right to have a preference. They made me be grateful just for the fact that I can become a parent.

A cousin of mine adopted as they had been trying for years to conceive their own but couldn't. A very good friend of mine has had 5 inseminations the last years. I think the number is 5, I have lost count. The worst part is that the last two initially worked and she got pregnant. But I guess it wasn't meant to be because in her first pregnancy she miscarried a week later and in the second one she had an embryo resorption. Another couple we know miscarried twice also. I have more examples but the above are enough I think.

My point is that a child is a blessing and a life changing event if you know how to live the experience. Boy or girl doesn't matter. You told me that you will cry if the doctor tells you that you have a boy when that time comes. I hope that the tears are going to be only tears of joy. I am sure that when you start feeling the changes in your body and the baby moving inside you, all you will care about will be that it is well and healthy.

I did just write this e-mail but I am not going to send it to you. As I was writing it, I got stressed and I don't want to do the same to you. In a few months you and your husband will start your own journey of a common life and a family. I will tell you in person or I will have you read it when I won't feel that I am going to cloud your thoughts.

Talk later,
Yiannis"

February 10ᵗʰ, 2011

Last night was a very difficult night, especially from 11pm till 3 am. We hardly got any sleep. Rena was in great pain, she had contractions and frequent diarrhea. She was dizzy and at times she phased out unable to communicate with me. I thought she was going to have the baby right there on our bed. When she would calm down for a while, I would run into the living room and start gathering all the things we need for the hospital. We hadn't experienced such intensity before.

I called the doctor around 2 am and I woke him up. I told him about all that and he said that we could head to the hospital to induce labor if we wanted. I got scared. No, I didn't just get scared, I was terrified! While that was what I wanted to hear from the doctor, when I actually heard it, something made me decide that it was still not the right time. It was very strange! I had my pregnant doctor wife in bed in pain and a doctor on the phone and I, the non-doctor, made the decision that we would wait for one more hour and if this labor simulation went on, we would leave for the hospital. Within the following hour, Rena's pains went away and she fell sound asleep.

Naturally, we visited the doctor today and he told us to think about the option of going in on Saturday the 12ᵗʰ to induce labor, since she is not coming on her own. He feels that Rena is putting herself through unnecessary strain by waiting for natural labor. But the decision is ours. Will we go in on Saturday or will we wait and go past the due date? It is up to Rena.

February 11ᵗʰ, 2011

– Good morning doctor. It's Rena..
– Good morning! How are you? What's up?

- I was thinking about what you told us yesterday and I think we should go in tomorrow.
- So you have made up your mind? Good for you…wise decision…don't strain yourself any more.
- Yeah, that's what I was thinking, too. I couldn't bear going through what I did the night before and not actually giving birth.
- Great! Don't worry about a thing! Let's meet tomorrow morning at 8 at the hospital. I will call and let them know we are coming.

While Rena was talking to the doctor, she walked up and down the kitchen. I was looking at her with my mouth and ears open. A few minutes before, she had got up and come to the kitchen where I was drinking my coffee. She told me about her decision to have our little girl on Saturday and I agreed. I told her to call the doctor right away.

After we talked to the doctor, we called our parents. They needed to get prepared and join us at the hospital. My parents were going to come over for dinner, anyway, so they planned on staying the night and coming with us in the morning.

Tomorrow! Tomorrow is the day we have been waiting for. We will see her little face, her tiny hands and feet. It seems incredible to me that we are almost there. There is baby fever in the house. There is a lot of excitement and a lot of nervousness. Tomorrow we will live extraordinary moments. We must rest to be able to cope and take in each and every one of them.

Tomorrow! Tomorrow defines today as the last day that Rena and I are going to be just the two of us.

Saturday, February 12th, 2011

end of week 39 beginning of week 40

It is 8 am and we came to the hospital an hour ago. My Rena is in a room getting prepared. My parents and I are waiting in the waiting area. My father-in-law is flying in from Samos and my mother-in-law is "stranded" in Samos. She is "stranded" in Samos for two reasons. The first one is that, unfortunately, her mother passed away a few days ago and tomorrow is the 9-day ceremony that is customary to take place after someone's death. The second reason is that she is sick and contagious. Therefore, she needs to stay away from all of us and especially from Rena and the baby. I have been thinking about her and I am sure that she is really hurting that she can't be here.

I keep looking at the door. I am waiting for the door to open and be called to go inside and join my wife. I guess the doctor is not here yet. If he were, we would have heard him. His voice is loud and characteristic. My parents and I engage in insignificant chit chat and I am doing my best to hide my nervousness. My poor parents, I have them carrying all our stuff, my bag with my netbook inside, the camera and the video camera, my jacket, Rena's papers and the baby's X-rays. I can't imagine how they are feeling; surely they are anxious for everything to go well. So what if this is their third granddaughter and their third time waiting in the delivery waiting area? They do have a lot of experience in this but I guess it doesn't matter. I don't even dare ask them how they are doing; it is still too early to get emotionally charged.

We are beginning to get sore sitting in the uncomfortable chairs in the waiting area. My mother is fantasizing about the sofas she noticed on the ground floor, big leather sofas that looked mighty comfortable. I told them to go upstairs on the ground floor after I go inside and I would come out later to get them up to speed.

"For Mrs Parassiris?", the lady nurse called out. I jump out of my chair and head towards the door they instructed me to go wait out from. The door opens and as it closed behind me I found myself in a small area between doors. A male nurse is waiting for me there and he helps me put on a robe that will cover my clothes. He also hands me a couple of plastic protective covers for my shoes. The second door opens and we enter the sterilized hall of labor and surgery rooms. There is a long reception desk in the middle of the room which reminds me of scenes from American series with dramatic stories that fold out in the hospital halls. There are also small rooms with big thick doors, all next to each other. Outside each room there is a sign depicting a pregnant lady laid on her back with a big round belly, ready to expose its content.

"Mrs Parassiris is in room 5", the nurse told me. From the first moment we walked into the hospital this morning, Rena's last name magically vanished form the registries. They use the last name that will be given to the child in order to avoid any misunderstandings and any confusing unfortunate incidents with the babies.

My wife is waiting for me in room number 5. They have already applied the epidural and the serum; she is already hooked up in the instrument that monitors the heartbeats of our child. She looks at me happy and relatively relaxed. Our midwife is with her, she has been here all along. I don't know exactly what is going on, what stage we are at. It is something to nine and I ask them to explain the procedure to me. The midwife tells me that she has already been administered the medication for inducing labor and she has already taken the painkillers, of course.

The doctor is not here yet and I am asking to find out

where he is. The midwife tells me that he will be here soon and not to worry because we won't be delivering the baby any time soon. "Oh really? When do you think?", I ask the midwife. "Early evening around 5 or 6." I was surprised. I wasn't expecting the whole process to take so long. My poor Rena, it's not going to be easy for her, lying back all those hours all wired up without being able to move around.

I leave Rena and the midwife in the room and I walk out to inform my parents of the situation. Our midwife is amazing. She is standing on Rena's bedside constantly as if she were her mother. She is very focused and in a very good mood. She has this paper that she every so often takes out of her pocket and reads jokes from it. Rena laughs her heart out. I love our midwife. Why? Because she makes my Rena laugh, I don't need another reason. Now, there are more people waiting outside. Aunts and uncles are here to stand by us. I insist that they go up on the ground floor to get seated on the comfortable sofas. "This is going to take longer than we had expected, you are going to get sore sitting here.". Rena's aunt is looking at me and her eyes are begging me for more information. "Come out more often and keep us updated, all right?" At that moment I realized that the people in the waiting area are in the dark about what is taking place in the delivery room, as opposed to me who is inside and I know that all is well. Being in the dark isn't a good felling. I promise them that I will come out every two hours to update them. Meanwhile, my father-in-law has arrived and is already inside with his daughter. His longing to be with his daughter was such that he quickly greeted everyone after he had stormed in the waiting lounge, literally threw his jacket to his sister to hold on to it, lied to the nurse that he is a doctor and got right in. He is indeed a doctor but when he told the nurse he said it in such a way that anyone would understand that he is a doctor working at this specific hospital. Good for him, I would have done the same! My parents take the rest of the group and head for the ground floor. I am so glad my parents are here. They give me a sense of security and confidence. They can't really do anything but it feels good to know that they are out there waiting and praying for the normal course of this delivery.

"I 'll see you all at noon then".

Going back inside and heading towards room 5, where my wife and my unborn daughter are waiting for me, I laugh with myself. I managed once more, even today, to organize myself and others and propose a schedule…"I will come out every two hours to update you".

Things in room 5 are moving along slowly and quietly with no intense pains and without much progress in the cervical dilation. I have already got used to the examination the midwife does to Rena every hour. She inserts her hand in…you know where…to check the centimeters that the cervix has opened. Behind there, our daughter with her little head is waiting to come out. The first time the midwife intruded my wife's vagina in this way, I almost passed out but I pushed myself not to and stood still. There was no way I would fall into the stereotype of the faint-hearted husband and miss out on all those magical moments. I also knew that they would throw me out if I showed any signs of weakness.

The doctor has arrived and he is chatting away with my father-in-law, they are very good friends. The doctor seems to me like a small God today, a small God that holds the fate of my family in his hands. He is tall and imposing, he has developed a fully-rounded stomach and, as I mentioned before, he has a loud, characteristic voice that makes him easily recognizable from many meters away. He is very reassuring and he's got a great sense of humor. He has contributed to the great mood that now exists in room 5, the room in which some of the most amazing scenes in our life will be played out.

I am on time for my noon appointment to update everyone and I go up to the ground floor cafeteria where I see the "girls". The "girls" are the cousins and friends of my wife who have all gathered to support their girlfriend. I bring them up to speed and I joke with them and tease them about the half-eaten sweets that I see on the table next to their coffees. I urge them to go home and come back in the evening. They tell me to give their best to Rena. I get up to leave as quickly as possible so as not to get emotional but from the corner of my eye I catch Maria looking at me, deep in my eyes. With her eyes wet and her voice trembling, she tells me "Tell her we are thinking about her…". I consider it a privilege to receive all this love and concern on behalf of my wife and I am obliged to express the girls' sentiments to her in as much accuracy as possible.

I meet my parents and the rest of the relatives on the ground floor's lounge. They are relaxing on the sofas. I have a strong espresso to get an energy boost. On the lounge's coffee table I can see the remains of my father's raid to the nearest convenience store, all sorts of junk food that we usually never consume. However, at times like these we find an excuse to indulge. I update everyone and again with their best wishes I head towards the basement to put on once again my sterilized hospital uniform.

The picture in room 5 hasn't changed that much. I am desperately trying to find some "alone" time with Rena to hold her hand more tenderly, to kiss her lips and tell her how much I love her. It is beyond me to find the right words to express my feelings for this woman who is in pain for the sole purpose of bringing the fruit of our love into this world. And what do I do? Nothing! I just stand there and look at her and I can do nothing. If only there was a way I could share her hardship and her pains. There isn't, though, and I think that from now on I will forever live with this burden that my guilt is creating. This is the guilt of utter uselessness and inability to actively participate in her ordeal. But maybe it is the guilt that will drive me to do the best I can for my family in the future. Maybe it is the guilt that will make me take on roles that Rena won't be able to in the future. Nature has endowed us with instincts and emotions that help us survive and live a better life. I accept them, if they are going to make me a better husband, a better father, a better man.

During the 2 o'clock news release appointment on the ground floor, I decide to eat something, too, in order to have strength to stand by my Rena. A turkey sandwich and some dark chocolate for dessert will do the job. I resist the salty temptations from the convenience store because they have nothing to offer me and they will most likely make me sleepy.

I wonder how my mother-in-law is doing back in Samos. Is anybody giving her the news? I call her without asking my father-in-law and her joy to hear me on the phone is indescribable. She has already talked to my father-in-law but she wants to hear more details from me. I tell her that everything is going well but slow. She sounds tired and worn out, obviously from crying her eyes out that she can't be there with us. She wants to know if her child, who is bringing her own child to life, is all right. "She is fine, don't worry, I will call you every couple of hours, when I come out".

The picture in room 5 is finally starting to change. The cervix has started dilating to the point that encourages us to think that progress is on the way. But Rena is in serious pain now. The epidural medication is not working and when it works it is only for a little while. From this point on, I can't recall many things. Rena's exhaustion and pains make everything else seem like a blurry picture.

I do remember intensely something that happened later in the evening when in the room there were our midwife, the hospital's midwife, a nurse and me. Rena was breathing heavily from the pains that she was in and all of a sudden I was pushed aside and asked to stay back as the midwives and the nurse were running towards Rena. They grabbed an oxygen mask and they placed it above her nose and mouth. All three of them stayed frozen still looking up at the heartbeat of the baby. A few seconds later, they sighed with relief and said "…it's all right now, don't worry…". It is redundant to say that I had turned white from fear and I lost all feeling in my legs. Watching the medical staff running towards Rena and putting on the oxygen mask, I thought, "This is not happening, my Rena is not living this, this is not happening". It's a good thing I was calm enough not to say a word and let them do their job. Later, they explained that Rena was in such pain that she wasn't able to breathe properly which, in turn, made the baby's heart rate slow down. That is why they had to supply her with oxygen.

The evening hours flowed in the same pattern. The anesthesiologist could not understand why the medication that she gave Rena did not work for more than half an hour. My father-in-law seemed to hold it together but he is not that good of an actor. The doctor seemed very thoughtful and probably wondered why the cervix didn't have the required dilation and why we were moving along so slowly. I kept going outside every two hours to keep my scheduled news appointment with the relatives and friends. When I was inside, all I could do is hold Rena's hand while I watched her lose her strength and her positive outlook. I wouldn't be able to stand for even two hours what she did for fifteen whole hours.

The only time that Rena was able to relax for a while was when the anesthesiologist gave her a really strong medicine to ease her pain. Within seconds she was sent to a world where the word "pain" does not exist in the dictionaries. She was so high that she kept smiling and asking our midwife if it was possible to "wrap some of that to take home". Although it made her feel good, it wasn't possible to keep receiving it because her muscles would relax so much that she wouldn't be able to push to give birth to our girl.

Much later in the evening the baby was ready to come out. It was in position and low enough to come out but the dilation wasn't enough to have Rena start pushing.

It was 10 pm and my Rena was so exhausted that she was having a difficult time perceiving things around her. I went out to talk to my father-in-law and the doctor. I found them discussing in a very serious tone.

- Doctor, what do you think?
- Well, look…we have dilation but it is moving along very slowly. It might be a good idea to…
- To have a caesarian section? Is it a good idea to have a caesarian? Rena is losing her strength and I don't see her being able to take any more of this.
- That will depend on you and Rena. A caesarian is a definite option at this point. What do you think Paraskevas?

My father-in-law was between a rock and a hard place as he was asked to help make a decision as a doctor and as a father. He was well aware of his daughter's wish to have a natural labor. On the other hand, he saw that the option of waiting even longer for natural birth could cause additional problems. Rena would probably not be strong enough to push the baby out and some other methods would have to be used to take it from her like forceps or vacuum extraction or something possibly harmful like that. He knew that the caesarian would require bed rest for at least two to three days but this is what we would end up doing anyway two or three hours from then. His opinion was to let things be for another hour and if there was no progress we would go ahead with the caesarian. We all agreed and I returned to room 5 to check on my wife.

As soon as I walked in, Rena, despite her exhaustion, could tell that I was gone for a while. She raised her head and asked me what took me so long and what we were discussing out in the hallway.

- What took so long? What were you guys talking about?
- Nothing, just talking...
- They are saying I should have a c-section, aren't they?
- Darling, it may be the best way to go right now. It is 10:30 and the dilation is not moving along. Can you take any more of this? Are you strong enough?
- No, I am not, not any more. Tell them I want to have the caesarian, I can't take this any longer!
- Are you sure, my love?
- Yes!
- All right, darling, I will tell the doctor. Would you like your father to be inside with you?
- Yes, ask him if he doesn't mind, I would feel more at ease.

I went out and headed towards the doctor and Rena's

father, thanking God on the way that Rena decided this on her own. I announced her decision and I told my father-in-law that she wanted him inside. I couldn't be with her because the c-section is actual surgery and only doctors are allowed to attend. The doctor gave the order and room 5 was flooded with nurses who started preparing Rena for the surgery. I asked our midwife if she would stay with her and she said she would, making me feel better.

"Do I have five minutes before I have to leave?", I asked the nurses, wishing they left the room to be alone with my wife before the surgery. Their response was positive but they didn't get the hint and stayed on in the room making the final preparations. I leaned over Rena and whispered in her ear.

- Everything is going to be all right, you know that baby, don't you?
- Yes, I do.
- I can't be in with you.
- I know, it's not allowed, we knew that.
- I know, but I wanted to be with you so much!
- You can't darling.
- Well, in a little while we will have our baby girl in our arms and your ordeal will be over.
- Yes.
- I love you baby!
- I love you, too!
- I will wait for you out in the lounge.
- Ok!
- I love you so much!
- Me, too!

Leaving the room, I was confident that Rena wasn't scared. It was quite clear to her that the c-section would redeem her from the pains. I was also confident because the doctor took me through the process and he made it sound very simple. I don't know if it actually is simple but I will suffice that he said so.

It was time for me to break the news to the friends and relatives. On the ground floor, the lounge was empty except for one part of it which was teeming with the people who were there on our account. In an armchair, far away from everyone else, I saw someone having fallen into a deep sleep, looking completely worn out. I got closer and saw that it was my father.

– Dad, wake up!
– What's up? How is Rena?
– Come inside with the others and I'll tell you.

I gathered everyone together and I told them that we had to do a caesarean because the cervix is not dilating as fast as it should have and Rena is losing her strength. Initially, most of them went pale. I reassured them by telling them that the process is simple and that she won't need to be fully sedated.

Everyone took their stuff and we headed to the basement. We camped outside the door that would open and we would see the baby and Rena. It was 11:30 pm.

I could not get myself to sit down so I kept pacing back and forth joking around with our friends. To distract everyone's attention, I asked Olga and her husband Aris to shoot with the video camera. I asked them to get comments and wishes from everyone for Rena, for a happy outcome. They all had something to say, the younger and calmer made jokes, especially Aris. The elders barely managed to hide their agony.

I didn't dare to be afraid. I didn't have that luxury.

For something to go wrong with Rena or the baby was not an option. There was no way I would get scared and stress out because everything would go perfect, it had to. Only momentarily did some bad thoughts go through my head but they disappeared as quickly as they appeared.

Then, I thought about my mother-in-law, back in Samos. I hadn't told her anything. I decided to call her after it was all finished so that she wouldn't have to go through the anxiety of the surgery on her daughter.

The time was close to midnight and everyone started betting on whether she would be born before midnight, therefore Saturday the 12th, or after midnight, therefore Sunday the 13th. They each said their piece of mind and justified their reasons why it would be better to be the 12th or the 13th.

- If she is born on a Saturday, she will be a Saturday-born and anything she says will come true.
- Yes, but if she is born on Sunday the 13th, she will be very lucky.

More of that followed until the time was ten minutes past midnight and the door opened. Oh God, I would see my child for the very first time. I could not believe that the time was here.

My father-in-law opened the door and with teary and glowing eyes he said to me: "Come and see your daughter!". I went inside the small, narrow room and behind me I could hear cries of happiness and admiration. I don't really remember any of that. All I remember is a buzz coming from them. Even that blurry buzz was completely muted when I saw my little daughter for the first time in my life in her little plastic container. A real-life, beautiful little creature covered in a tiny blanket which the midwife opened to show me her trembling little body. The hospital midwife was talking to me giving me the details like the time of birth, 11:50 pm, the weight, 3,150 kilos. Her lips kept moving but I wasn't listening. Her words had become incomprehensible mumbles that meant nothing to me. I looked at my little one, still with happiness and as I was trying to get over the first shock and not feel numb any more, my mother had leaned over and was talking to her. My daughter was looking at her with wide-open eyes and she was crying. You would call it more of a mewing than crying. Her little chin was going up and down from the cold and she was crying so elegantly, so girly. Her eyes were black and almond-shaped, the exact same shape as her mother's. I was hoping for that, to get Rena's eyes. Her hair was black, like her grandfather's, Rena's dad. Her nose and cheeks, those she got from me.

Before I take the baby in my arms, I looked at my father-in-law and I asked him if Rena was all right. I could hear my own voice shaking. He nodded that she was fine and I tried to discern in his eyes or his voice if he was hiding something from me. He wasn't.

The midwife asked me to stretch my arms forward and wrapped me up in a blanket. Then she placed our little angel in my arms. It was as if the skies had opened and God Himself had handed me over this gorgeous baby! She was so light, so vulnerable and so very beautiful! When I held her, I began talking to her. She instantly stopped crying and looked deep into my eyes.

"Welcome my love…my heart! We have been waiting for you for so long and now you are here. Yes, my baby, now you are here!…What is it darling? Yes, it's me, your daddy, that voice you have been hearing all this time along with your mummy's. My sweetheart, you are so beautiful, just like we were expecting you to be. You have your mother's eyes and they are so beautiful. You had a hard time coming out, didn't you baby? Yes, you did, you are right. But you are here now. It's me baby, it's daddy! And I will love you for ever!"

The midwife was trying to take her out of my arms and I was not paying her any attention. "I have to take her now to get her cleaned and dressed. We will bring her to you later in the room". She finally convinced me to let her go.

«Go now darling and I will see you in a little bit. My baby girl!"

When I walked out of the room, dazed from my first contact with the baby, I was trying to find a chair to sit down. When I did, I collapsed. I stuck my face in my hands and I was crying incessantly, relieved that everything went so well. I couldn't talk to anyone. My mother was standing next to me with a bottle of water, just in case, and was lightly stroking my shoulder. My father came and stood right in front of me, put his hands under my armpits, lifted me up and hugged me tight, to make me feel safe and secure. I felt as if I was five years old and what he did felt so welcoming to me. Then, followed my mother's more tender hug. After that, I was ready to accept everyone's wishes.

About fifteen minutes later, they brought Rena to the little, narrow room. They called me inside to see her. She was lying back and her eyes were wet and shiny and…huge! I had never seen her eyes like that before. She was looking at me so intensely that I felt like two bright rays of light were piercing through me. She was looking at me with such love that, once again, she made me feel very privileged.

"Did you see her?", she asked me with tired enthusiasm.

"I saw her my love, she is perfect!".

I leaned over and kissed her on the cheek. "She is gorgeous, darling, and so healthy. Congratulations, baby, you did such a good job all these months…I love you so much!" Besides my parents who walked in to see her and congratulate her, I asked her if she wanted to see the others but she couldn't handle it. Just when the door was closing, she turned her head to see if all the "girls" were there. The "girls" got a split second chance to wave their hands from the crack of the door. .

They took Rena away, too. The next meeting of the three of us would be in the room. The Parassiris family would meet up again on the sixth floor.

This diary ends here. It ends because I am not "about" to be a dad any more. I am a dad!

A new exciting, magical trip begins, one with more surprises and more challenges. From now on, the rest of our lives will be defined by the fact that we have the divine privilege of being parents!

Welcome to our world little baby! Know that we will love you very much!

Welcome our child!